For you
harvesting

The Cry of the Harvest

by Chad Taylor

D1065894

Xulon PRESS

www.xulonpress.com

Endorsements

Chad is a new breed of evangelist. He is able to repro-duce his perspective in the reader and give an insatiable hunger for seeing people come into the full invitation of salvation. Chad not only has a fresh way of thinking that is full of life, he also has an appetite to give his best so that we can benefit from his expertise and heart.

—Shawn Bolz
Author of *Keys to Heaven's Economy*
and *The Throne Room Company*

Chad Taylor addresses the greatest issue on the heart of God right now—the harvest. He does so with profound insight and prophetic stirring. I highly recommend this evan-gelistic gem.

—Bill Johnson
Pastor, Bethel Church
Redding, California.

The prevailing spirit or tone of Chad Taylor's newest book could be summed up in one word—passion! I believe the Lord of the harvest is stirring His church to once again respond to His mandate to go into *all* the world, and Chad seems to be vastly ahead of the rest of us in this area. It is time for the bride to put feet to her beliefs and fulfill the Great Commission. Chad's done it in his life, and now it's time for the rest of us to follow his example. I was deeply challenged. Good job, Chad!

—Dennis Cramer
Dennis Cramer Ministries

Chad Taylor truly reflects the Heart of God for the lost people of our time. This book will cause one to feel uncomfortable with 'normal' and passionate about the 'harvest'. The harvest was the mission of Jesus and the request he made to His followers to pray for the Lord to send laborers into the harvest. When you read this book many will be moved from spectators to harvesters for the Glory of God. Thanks Chad for staying faithful to the historic trail of true evangelist through the centuries which began with Jesus our Lord.

— Arthur Blessitt
Arthur Blessitt Ministries

The Cry of the Harvest is right in time with what God is doing today. Chad Taylor's heart for touching people with God's love is contagious. Let this book ignite a fire of new hope within you to reach a generation for Jesus!

—Doug Addison
InLight Connection

Dedication

I humbly dedicate this humble work to the late Leonard Ravenhill and Keith Green. It was Leonard's letters, phone calls and face-to-face prayers that helped bring these words into the light. It was the music and message of Keith Green that continues to stir and move my heart toward an upward call in Christ Jesus. I pray that the cry for harvest does not fall on deaf ears; but rather burns like molten lava on the indifference of religion and mobilize a great end-time army that loves the Lord of the Harvest...

We Christians are debtors to all men at all times in all places, but we are so smug to the lostness of men. We've been "living in Laodicea," lax, loose, lustful, and lazy. Why is there this criminal indifference to the lostness of men? Our condemnation is that we know how to live better than we are living.

—Leonard Ravenhill

Contents

Acknowledgments

I would like to thank the many contributors and friends who have made this book a reality. The team of harvesters and prayer warriors at Solomon's Rest in Bismarck, North Dakota, were invaluable. Thank you for your priceless contribution to this project!

Geneva Childers of Georgia, your tireless support will never go unnoticed, and I will always count you as a friend and fellow soldier on the front lines.

Sheri Lopez, modern missionary, confidante, and friend, your relentless commitment to the gospel has inspired me to write this book to see an army of evangelists, such as yourself, raised up and sent out. Keep fighting the good fight of faith!

The small ragtag, far-flung supporters over the years who have supported Consuming Fire via the Internet, I am in debt to you in Christ. Your small but persistent donations, epic prayers, and unshakable commitment to the cause have inspired me to continue, no matter the cost.

And to you, the reader, the treasure out of religion's darkness, I pray that this book inspires you to greater works and distant shores as you commit your life completely to the call. It's for you I write. Even as Paul said long ago, "But I want you to know, brethren, that the things which happened to me have actually turned out for the furtherance of the gospel" (Phil. 1:12).

Introduction

In every revival, there is a reemphasis of the church's missionary character. Men return to Calvary, and the world is seen afresh through the eyes of Christ. The infinite compassion of Christ fills the heart, and the passion evoked by Calvary demands the whole wide world as the fruit of His sacrifice.

—John Shearer

In this late hour, a new breed of missionary shall be heard over the din of contemporary clamor. They shall shout as they shouted on the plains of Jericho, and the walls of religious restraint shall fall from them. Traditional armor will be shed for a more undignified approach. They will surprise hell with their unconventional tactics, and the spoil of nations will be left at their feet.

They will be like the four lepers at the gates of the city, who will exclaim, "If we sit here, we will die!" They will come to the awesome conclusion that modern methods have failed, and they will arrive at the river of a new experience and select five smooth stones. They will discover the momentum of harvest and fling themselves at the giants of the age as their predecessor David did. They will be a dangerous dilemma to hell as they poise themselves in the fields by night as the shepherds of old did, and the heavens will be opened to them.

The mild-mannered methods of modern ministry will not take hold of these. They will thunder across the land with a cry of harvest. They will come upon a city, like lightning, to leave the forest of men's thinking in ashes. They will walk like Elijah did and call down fire on the altars of intellectualism and enlightenment. Nations will turn at the sight of this burning. Kings will issue decrees at the sight of these, this new breed. The lion's den of religious persecution will produce these modern-day Daniels. They will come with a message of heaven for a planet void of it.

They will be a Joseph in times of spiritual famine, famine from hearing the Word of God. They will be the youth who survive the fires of men's thinking to emerge from the institutions without even the hint of smoke on their clothes. They will dress different, act different, sleep different. They will raise a standard of holiness not defined by outward religious acts but rather the hidden man of the heart. They will rewrite the theological pages of history with the tongue of a ready writer. Their words will be gold in a land of imitation.

The limitations of doctrine will not capture their hearts in fear. They will defy theories and the theorists of their time to reshape the minds of men. They will be the force that endures tribulation and prepares an army for war. They will confront the icons of theology and cast down the altars of escapism, and teach an army to fight the good fight of faith.

They have no comeliness that one would be drawn to them. But they will represent the faces of thousands of broken hearts, a voice for the voiceless and an advocate to those appointed to death. They know only one thing: "For the King and His kingdom..." He must increase in their ministries, and they must decrease. They do not look for the role of leader but are not afraid to lead. They are the forerunners to the greater works. They will set a prophetic precedent that will allow a generation of uncomely parts to enter the promised land.

They are living martyrs who have died already. They have lost their lives to gain His; they are crucified with Christ. It is not they who live, but Christ who lives in them. They have lost all identity in exchange for His authority. They are the Esthers of their day who comprehend that they were born for such a time as this. They will lose themselves to gain Him.

They will appear for a little while, and then you will see them no more. Like Philip in the Acts of the apostles, they will be "caught away" and disappear into other harvest fields to sow and reap. They will have no resting place on this earth; their kingdom is one to come. They march to a different drum. They will separate themselves from a system of temporary position and discard titles and trophies. They will refuse the kingly robes of reputation and will put on Christ. "The earth quakes before them, the heavens tremble; the sun and moon grow dark, and the stars diminish their brightness. The Lord gives voice before His army, for His camp is very great" (Joel 2:10–11).

Chapter 1

This Great Harvest

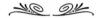

The Great Commission is not an option to be considered; it is a command to be obeyed.

—Hudson Taylor

When Jesus said, "The harvest is plentiful," He wasn't practicing some allegorical phraseology—it was an absolute truth. Let's take a moment to see how great this harvest really is. In A.D. 1 when Christ walked this earth, there were approximately 150 million people. As Jesus surveyed the world from Calvary, this is what He saw and died for. He also saw into the near future when the world population, or harvest, would exponentially take a quantum leap into the billions. Jesus stated that the harvest is plentiful but the workers are few when there were only150 million people in the earth's population. Imagine what that word *few* means now with over 6 billion people?

In February of 2006, we reached the 6.5 billion mark and are expected to reach 8 billion by 2020. Yes, that's right—8 billion by 2020. Our harvest is not only plentiful, but it's overwhelming. The world population increased from 3 billion in 1959 to 6 billion by 1999, doubling over a forty-year span. The world population is projected to grow from the 6 billion in 1999 to 9 billion by 2042, an increase of 50 percent (wikipedia.org). Are you reeling yet?

Jesus must have seen this through the portal of time and space when He exclaimed, "Therefore pray the Lord of the harvest to send out laborers into His harvest" (Matt. 9:38). This was a very prophetic statement, as the Creator of the universe, from His eternal vantage point, saw a world not decreasing in number and thus making it much easier to reach, but rather increasing! His prophetic prayer for laborers was profound and still is the quintessential prayer of the age.

In 2006 alone, we had 132,434,587 births and 55,220,152 deaths. Of those who died, how many knew Jesus Christ as their friend and Lord? Someone is born every 4.2 seconds and dies every 1.8 seconds. Evangelism and world harvest are literally a moment-by-moment, second-by-second injunction that must begin to take priority, or billions will face the possibility of not coming to the saving knowledge of Jesus Christ.

Even more harrowing than these numbers are the tragic words that Jesus declared as He viewed the vast expanse of human existence with its ebb and flow of life and death: "But the laborers are few." (Luke 10:2). Jesus saw the rise and fall of generations that would detour from His Great Commission, thus leaving an immense vacuum of souls. As we face the horizon of humanity and the doubling of the human population, there has never been a better time to seize the prayer of Jesus and intercede for the laborers to be released and reap a harvest that is becoming more plentiful by the second.

Statistics tell us that currently 3,354,608,348 people have not had an adequate presentation of the gospel of Jesus Christ. That, my friend, is half the world's population! The mirage that presents the world as a saved one is an illusion that must be shattered so that this present generation of Christians will rise up from the fog of false peace and give their lives to the defense of the gospel.

The two largest harvest fields in the world are China, with a population of 1,306,313,812, and then India, with 1,080,264,388. India is projected to pass China in population by 2050. In a distant third as the most populated nation in the world is the United States, with 295,734,134 million souls. These numbers are staggering, but if the tens of hundreds of millions who claim to be born-again Christians obeyed the command of Jesus to go into all the world and preach the gospel, it could be accomplished. God impacted and changed the world with much less in the first century; what is the problem now? Numbers are not God's problem, but the willingness to sacrifice and commit are.

This is a graphic picture of the harvest that Jesus prophesied is plentiful and ready, but how many are heeding these numbers and statistics? We must have a fresh wave of new missionaries, both young and old, to recommit their lives to the cross. Without this great commitment, we will never obey the Great Commission. I said, *Without this great commitment, we will never obey the Great Commission!*

Read the vision of Loren Cunningham, the founder of Youth with a Mission. This vision has not come to its complete fulfillment yet, but I believe we are on the precipice of its becoming a reality now.

That night after our singing engagement, I returned to the missionary's guest room with its white walls, unadorned except for an island scene in a cheap wooden frame. I lay down on the bed, doubled the pillow under my head, and opened my Bible, routinely asking God to speak into my mind. What happened next was far from routine. Suddenly, I was looking up at a map of the world—only, the map was alive, moving! I sat up. I shook my head, rubbed my eyes. It was a mental movie. I could see all the continents. Waves were crashing onto the shores. Each went onto a continent, then receded, then came up farther until it covered the continent completely. I caught my breath. Then, as I watched, the scene changed. The waves became young people–kids my age and even younger–covering the continents. They were talking to people on the street corners and outside bars. They were going house to house. They were preaching. (Into All the World by Loren Cunningham)

This next missionary thrust will not only crash upon the shores of foreign countries and obscure villages, but upon the sets and back lots of Hollywood and MTV. A new breed of missionary is taking center stage, with a prophetic creativity that will transcend modern interpretations of art and music and display the kingdom of God. They will be the modern Josephs who interpret the hungry hearts of a generation and become an ensign of the endtimes. We must pray now like never before for their coming out and that the curtains of modern church will not remain closed to their entrance. We must embrace this new breed of ministers who shine in a world filled with gross darkness. They are not conformed to previous methodology and standards but are setting a new precedent of creativity and power. This great end-time harvest that Jesus defined in Mathew 13:39 is upon us, and a new missionary thrust marked by unparalleled signs and wonders will follow. Lord, here am I; send me!

Chapter 2

Do the Work of an Evangelist

*If sinners be damned, at least let them leap to hell
over our bodies. If they will perish, let them perish
with our arms about their knees. Let no one go there
unwarned and unprayed for.*

— C. H. Spurgeon

The word *evangelist, euangelistes* in the Greek, literally means "a messenger of good," "preacher of the gospel," or "to proclaim glad tidings." Also, *euangelistes* means "a messenger similar to an angel," "to announce good news," "to proclaim glad tidings," and "to declare." Evangelism is the vocal cords of the gospel, the shout of the kingdom, and the trumpet blast of heaven.

Often we recognize the prophet as the mouthpiece of eternity, but in light of New Testament revelation, the evangelist has taken his place. As we see in Acts 8, it was an evangelist who blazed the trail for the apostolic and prophetic and laid the foundation for the Samaritan church. Philip was a prototype of a prophetic evangelism that would change the face of the church forever.

It was declared in Acts 21:8, "Philip the evangelist." If you read further, it makes reference to the daughters of

Philip, "which did prophesy." Philip was not only an evangelist, but he was also a *prophetic evangelist* infused with New Testament power and anointing. He was not classified as a fivefold minister, but rather he was a New Testament revivalist who produced prophetic fruit and transformed entire regions with the gospel. Philip was a messenger of good, a preacher of the gospel, and proclaimed glad tidings.

Evangelism is the catalyst for miracles, signs, and wonders. Evangelism is the hinges of the apostolic. Without it the church will not grow and does not expand. When Philip arrived in Samaria, they "heard and saw the miracles which he did" (Acts 8:6). Without evangelism the world cannot *hear* or *see* the message of Christ. In all thy getting, get evangelism!

The apostolic exhortation to the infant church of the first century was clear: "Do the work of an evangelist" (2 Tim. 4:5). Or, in other words, announce good news, declare boldly, and go as a messenger or ambassador of the gospel. It means to proclaim the kingdom of God and heal the sick, raise the dead, and cast out demons. Evangelism was the engine that moved the message of Jesus Christ and compelled the vehicle of ministry. It was never intended for an elite company of radical young people, but rather it was the mandate for *all* the church from then until now.

Also, according to the Greek, missionaries are evangelists. They are apostolic "sent ones" who hasten the coming day of God. They are the green light of heaven that invites angels en masse to conquer strongholds and release the captives. They hold the key that unlocks every prison door and releases all of them that are bound. They are the shod feet of intercession that carries His glory and answers every prayer.

The moment Jesus declared to the apostles to "go into the entire world and preach the gospel to every creature" (Mark 16:15), the revival anointing was released. He promised to work with them, confirming the Word with signs following. This mighty anointing for revival and reformation is now available to every Christian. It is not a limited resource exclusive to full-time ministers and TV evangelists; it's the mandate and mission of the timeless body of Christ. It is you, and it is I.

We must begin to pray that the great well of evangelism would be opened again. It is the endless well that produced the messages of Billy Sunday and Billy Graham catapulting millions into hostile environments. These wells have been obstructed with the stones of tradition and indifference but are now being reopened by the hands of a restless, unsatisfied generation that will not partake in the regurgitated rhetoric of contemporary religion. They carry the DNA of Philip, the prophetic evangelist, and Paul, the apostolic evangelist. They carry the same mandate as Paul: "My ambition has always been to preach the Good News where the name of Christ has never been heard, rather than where a church has already been started by someone else" (Rom. 15:20 NLT).

Chapter 3

The Modern-Day Missionary

If a commission by an earthly king is considered an honor, how can a commission by a heavenly king be considered a sacrifice?
— David Livingstone

The heart that compels a person to abandon all earthly endeavors for unseen borders and foreign fields is still the driving force of the gospel. It defined the life of Jesus as He declared to the crowd, "I must preach the kingdom of God in other cities also: for this reason was I sent" (Luke 4:43). The call of God could never be confined to one location, as it was always bursting the seams of longitude and latitude. It is the same Spirit who captures the imagination of a child to dream of faraway places and strange lands. It is the same force that unsettles and displaces our idea of stability and security and causes us to uproot and go to build, plant, and expand His kingdom.

Today's missionaries can be seen not only in obscure villages in forgotten parts of the world but in metropolitan empires, homespun coffee shops, shopping centers and malls, skateboard parks, sporting arenas, and in every other form of public venue. They have been called outside the paradigm of current Christianity that orbits around the epicenter of architectural wonders, and they find their energy and spirituality in the wafting air of the city street.

The conveyor belt of Christianity, with its rituals and rites, repels them into a lifestyle that is contagious and evangelistic. They are a new breed of missionary, with briefcase, skateboard, laptop, and all other sorts of modern paraphernalia in tow. They can dress in suits or Billabong shorts and surf the North Shore of Oahu. The world is their stage, and they view the wide-open land as their harvest. They are unstoppable, and their fervency for faraway places yet undefined by modern church drives them.

These evangelists enlist the help of local buses and city transit, allowing them to find every nook and cranny of their city, seeking out the lost, lonely, and bedraggled. With Bible in tow, they can find windows of opportunity everywhere they go. The blood of the missionary burns in their veins, and every sidewalk, airplane, sporting arena, and mecca of civilization becomes their mission field. The epoch of shopping malls with their endless stores and food courts is transformed before their eyes into vast marketplaces where the harvest is waiting to be reaped.

Is this you? Do you step from your doorway into a field waiting to be reaped, or is the gravity of routine still holding you? Ask the Holy Spirit to brand you with the same anointing that compelled Paul when he penned these words: "For though I preach the gospel, I have nothing to glory of; for necessity is laid upon me, yes, woe is me if I preach not the gospel" (1 Cor. 9:16). Ask the Lord to infix upon your heart the same necessity that compelled Paul to travel endless miles and endure every possible resistance until you, too, can say, "Woe is me if I do not preach the gospel."

Despite every inadequacy and inability, the plumb line of His Word is inside, waiting for you to step out. As you stand at the crossroads of your comfort zone and the harvest beyond it, read these words carefully: "For it is not you that speaks but the Spirit of your Father that speaks through you" (Matt. 10:20). You are simply a willing conduit and vehicle that He can express His power and love through. Once you leap the hurdle of self, the world awaits you. Listen to how Paul put it: "And I, brethren, did not come to you with excellent speech or wisdom declaring to you the testimony of God.... My speech and preaching was not with enticing words of man's wisdom but rather in the demonstration of God's power so that your faith would not stand in the wisdom of man but *in the power of God*" (1 Cor. 2:1–5, emphasis added). You, my friend, can do it!

You are God's modern-day missionary with a plethora of advantages at your fingertips. For a mere few hundred dollars, you can travel to another country and partner with teams around the world preaching the gospel of Jesus Christ. Your life is a masterpiece waiting to be created, full of adventure and excitement as the Holy Spirit paints with broad strokes of your future.

Take a firm grip on the plow and never look back, and suddenly your self-worth will skyrocket as you realize you are a colaborer with Christ. He stands hand in hand with you in the harvest field. In the twinkling of an eye, you are in rank and number with thousands before you who have made history in their missionary endeavors around the world. You are God's anointed! The moment you step out, take a deep breath and plunge into the depths of possibility.

Chapter 4

The Baptism of Jesus

*Some wish to live within the sound of a chapel bell; I
wish to run a rescue mission within a yard of hell.*
—C. T. Studd

"John came baptizing in the wilderness and preaching a
baptism of repentance for the remission of sins. Then
all the land of Judea, and those from Jerusalem, went out
to him and were all baptized by him in the Jordan River,
confessing their sins" (Mark 1:4–5). When Jesus stepped
into the muddied water of the Jordan, it was much more than
a symbolic gesture to the law. All the people of the land of
Judea and Jerusalem had been immersed in the river, leaving
behind the grime and dirt of daily living. No outhouses or
other modern conveniences waited for them, only the slow-
moving waters of the Jordan. It wasn't until innumerable
crowds of men, women, and children had been baptized in
the river and waded along the shallow shoreline that Jesus
finally put His feet into the water. Even more intense than
the smell of the masses was the immeasurable weight of sin
left swirling in the current as well. You see, Jesus was not
just practicing a religious ritual when He told John to baptize
Him—He was immersing Himself in the smell and sin of

all the people. The spotless Lamb lay in the watery grave of Israel's sin and led the way to resurrection.

It was no surprise then when John cried in dismay, "I need to be baptized by You, and are You coming to me?" Another significant sign is the fact that Jesus' anointing was first visible at the Jordan and not at another more notable and holy landmark. It was at the basest of places that Jesus began to contradict the mighty and wealthy. God is still yearning to baptize a generation with this unrivaled anointing, but they must first immerse themselves into their own Jordan and consider this calling. God is still looking for one who will avoid the iconic and hypnotic sway of men's acceptance and wade into the white water of this world and let Him sweep them away.

> "For you see your calling, brethren, that not many wise according to the flesh, not many mighty, not many noble, are called. But God has chosen the foolish things of the world to put to shame the wise, and God has chosen the weak things of the world to put to shame the things which are mighty; and the base things of the world and the things which are despised God has chosen, and the things which are not, to bring to nothing the things that are" (1 Cor 1:26–28).

Contemporary standards of ministry have often left a generation disoriented and disillusioned with the picture of elaborate ordinations and neatly framed certificates on paneled walls. Nothing could have been further from the truth in Jeremiah's day when the very hand of God touched him, sending him to the nations. Jeremiah must have faced a similar mind-set when he cried, "Ah, Lord God! Behold, I cannot speak, for I am a youth." This present population of Christians must embrace this call as well: "Before I formed you in the womb I knew you; before you were born I sanctified you; I ordained you a prophet to the nations" (Jer. 1:5–6).

It was no coincidence then that shortly after this baptism, Jesus began to heal *all* who were sick and demon-possessed throughout the regions where He was baptized. He had to get into a position where He could actually feel their needs and be a high priest who was in all points tempted as they were, yet without sin.

Do you want to have a greater impact on those around you? Then answer the call of Jesus: "Jesus said to them, 'You will indeed drink the cup that I drink, and with the baptism I am baptized with, you will be baptized' " (Mark 10:39–40). We, too, must step off the porches of current religious expectation and stir the water, and be the answer to the man at the pool of Bethesda who proclaimed, "I have no man to put me into the pool when the water is stirred up" (John 5:7). No man to put him into the pool? *When will the church begin to do what the angels are compelled to do in our absence?* Lord, in all Thy stirring, stir us!

Shortly after this, Jesus went to the wedding of Cana. Again we see Jesus breaking social and religious barriers and invading the world around Him. From these kinds of encounters, the greatest miracles were performed. The baptism of the Holy Spirit and fire is closely related to the baptism of Jesus in the Jordan: "I indeed baptize you with water unto repentance, but He who is coming after me is mightier than I.... *He will baptize you with the Holy Spirit and fire"* (Luke 3:16). The baptism of power awaits those who will enter the arena of human experience and engage people there. The dividing line of indifference will be shattered by those who follow the simple steps of Christ into their own Jordan and receive the baptism of power.

Today there is an invisible line of demarcation that insulates Christianity from the world. It has created its own baptism into a ready-made environment of Christian symbols, language, and an endless parade of events. We could live a thousand lifetimes attempting to attend all the conferences and seminars and yet never see the Jordan from the position of Jesus' baptism. We stand on the banks of human existence in all of its dirt, mud, and shame, never willing to step into it ourselves. Those willing to be baptized into the baptism of Christ will also share in His impact and fruit. The great statement of the Lord "Greater works shall you do" still awaits a generation that will step into the murky water of the Jordan and live it. Is it you?

Paul must have known this too when he penned these words: "To the weak became I as weak, that I might gain the weak: I am made all things to all men, that I might by all means save some" (1 Cor 9:22). Paul touched the Jew and the Gentile and longed to see Christ become a reality in all of them. It was this lifelong posture in His ministry that caused many to question His teaching and doctrine. Even today religious peer pressure disqualifies many from evangelism and soul winning with this rhetoric: "You are not trained," or "You are not ordained." Training is good, but training that leads to the merry-go-round of church attendance is not.

We need another seventy sent out two by two who return with joy reporting, "Lord, even the demons are subject to us in Your name!" (Luke 10:17). We need an army of Philips who ignore current trends and invade the modern marketplaces of the occult and the new age, risking their lives and reputations for revival. The eyes of the Lord are still searching the earth for those not content to orbit in the gratuitous gravity of today's popular trends, who follow a road less traveled where the footprints of former revivalists once tread. They are the parents of the greater works, who will witness not only crusades and benchmark events but entire nations saved and shaken. The hand of the clock is pointing to that moment in eternity, but the question still remains: *Will it be you?*

Chapter 5

The Prayer of Necessity, Not Convenience

Give me one hundred preachers who fear nothing but sin and desire nothing but God, and I care not a straw whether they be clergymen or laymen; such alone will shake the gates of hell and set up the kingdom of heaven on Earth.

—John Wesley

When Moses uttered those timeless words, "Show me Your glory," it was a prayer driven by necessity, not convenience. The hostile desert of Egypt was behind him, and an unknown vast expanse of land before him. The *kabod,* or glory, of God would be the only thing to sustain them in the midst of violent uprisings, armed attacks, and an endless array of opposition as they preserved His Word in a godless world. To them the glory of God was their survivability rather than a secret ingredient to success or fame. *It was the mark upon them that they were sent by God and not by man.*

The *kabod,* or glory, of God was to clothe a people in His manifest presence so that they would be a people set apart, different, full of power and wisdom, witnessing that He was God. Moses cried out, "If your presence does not go with me, then do not take us out of this place" (Exod. 33:15). Moses knew his only hope for success was the glory of God. It was the signature of the divine that they were not mere human vehicles carrying such precious cargo, but rather they were sent by God. Without it they were doomed to a world of destitution and decay, forever wandering outside the borders of their previous captivity, and Moses knew it. God's presence was not a spiritual spotlight that would line their pockets with gold, but to the contrary, it was the only option in a world that wanted them dead. Moses prayed a prayer of desperation.

It was the glory of God that kept David alive as Saul and his army pursued him through the treacherous mountains. It was the glory of God that shut the mouths of lions as Daniel cried out to God from his pit. It was the glory of God that preserved Paul in prisons, shipwrecks, and harrowing moments of life and death, allowing him to preach the gospel to far-flung places.

The glory of God was not a trivial manifestation that attracted the curious, but rather it was the shadow of the Almighty that burst open the doors to prison cells and shook entire cities. The glory of God was the harbinger of hope to colonies of lepers and scattered Christians marked for arrest, torture, and death. It was never a license for excess and extravagance; it was the key that unlocked the heavy stocks of incarceration and propelled the kingdom of God at light speed, setting the captives free.

In Acts 8, we see the clash of contradicting forces as two manifestations of spiritual power collide. Philip entered the borders of Samaria, preaching Jesus Christ with signs and wonders of healing, deliverance, and salvation. On the other hand, a local sorcerer was seducing the people with other "signs and wonders," masquerading as some power from

God. Look more closely at this spiritual battle in the city of Samaria: "But there was a certain man, called Simon, which beforetime in the same city used sorcery, and bewitched the people of Samaria, giving out that himself was some great one: to whom they all gave heed, from the least to the greatest, saying, This man is the great power of God. And to him they had regard, because that of long time he had bewitched them with sorceries" (Acts 8:9–11).

Entire cities were won, not only by God's power through the preaching of Jesus Christ, but also through sorcery and deceptive signs and wonders. On the stage of world harvest, the dividing line between the power of God and the subtle, strange smell of sorcery will be evident as it attempts to replace the simplicity of Jesus Christ and His confirming miracles that accompany the gospel message. No longer is it the *kabod* of God, but we see another glory, a glory reeking of a temporal, visible experience that brings the people immediate satisfaction.

Jesus was God's glory in the flesh, and yet He still had His Gethsemane. Nothing Jesus did or accomplished was without pain, prayer, and pressure. His glory was born in the furnace of affliction and "though He were a son, yet He learned obedience by the things He suffered" (Heb. 5:8). Paul taught the early churches of Lystra, Iconium, and Antioch that through much tribulation they would enter the kingdom of God. Through the vise of faith and suffering, they would apprehend a greater glory, and it would squeeze the aroma of Jesus from them to a lifeless world.

What a contrast to today's teaching that tells us the road to glory is an easy one with no pitfalls or pressure! We want to fast forward through Gethsemane, the cross, and Golgotha to a field full of flowers and resurrection bliss. How easy it is to nonchalantly turn the page to something more appealing when we read the powerful words of Paul to the Philippians: "That I may know him, and the power of his resurrection, and the fellowship of his sufferings, being made conformable unto his death" (Phil. 3:10).

The road to Ichabod is an easy one in all its fancy, outward appeal; the path to His glory, however, that arrests whole cities with signs, wonders, and power is a severe one that will ask nothing less than your life, reputation, and ambitions. Nothing, no matter how extravagant, can replace prayer and the preaching of His Word. With all the known world in a state of moral and spiritual upheaval, and despite the fact that even from within their own ranks the church was pressed on all sides, the severity of this shone through: "But we will give ourselves continually to prayer and the ministry of the word" (Acts 6:4).

The prayer closets have been abandoned for prayer lines where the conveyor belt of Christianity spits out spiritual gifts at blurring speed. The cry of salvation in the streets has been brushed aside for conferences and meetings where the poor and needy are turned away. The glory of God that is coming will not be an anesthetic but an alarm waking the watchman and sending His servants out quickly into the highways and the byways.

When Satan took Jesus up an "exceedingly high mountain and showed Him all the kingdoms of this world *and the glory of them,*" (Matt. 4:8) something was vastly different from when Moses ascended a similar mountain to see God's face and cry out for His glory. The first was a glory that promised immediate satisfaction; the latter was the rarefied glory of God that parted the Red Sea and made a way to lead a people into liberty and salvation.

Two mountains loom ahead of this current generation of Christians, and the appeal for the quick and costless will be powerful. Only the heart that really desires the heart of the Father and His insatiable desire to see a world saved will press through to a road less traveled. The landscape will be filled with alluring devices to draw us away from the promise of His true glory and presence that results in the harvest of souls that Jesus claimed on the cross.

Today we see another ascent up another mountain to find a different glory that fills the room with sweet smells and strange things. It's a glory that costs nothing and is worth even less. It attracts a crowd of people who do not carry the scars of Christ and are even more unwilling to go out into the world where these scars are earned. This place will never demand that a people take up their cross, deny themselves, and follow Jesus. It's a man-made edifice that's filled with terraces, tapestries, and trappings elaborately elegant in their outward appeal, but devoid of blood, sweat, and tears. Thus it will never produce a harvest, despite all its claims of joy and extravagance.

But from the smoke and mirrors of current movements and trends is emerging an army of uncompromised lovers of the cross. They are branded by persecution and have paid the price while many that they have known and loved have sold out to lesser things. They will be brands of fire plucked from the kindled altar of God's passion for revival and catalysts for a world ablaze with His knowledge and truth. They will be an unstoppable force tearing through popular trends and putting Christ on public display in the streets and lanes of the city. They will have the DNA of eternity, which reads, "It is not God's will that any man perish, but that all come to repentance." The nations of the world will be their objective as they rebuild a broken-down cross askew with modernism and religion.

Is this you? Does your heart burn inside as you read this? Then to the front lines of prayer and commitment as the Spirit of God baptizes you in a new, vital anointing to "heal the sick, cleanse the lepers, raise the dead, cast out devils; freely you have received, freely give" (Matt. 10:8).

Chapter 6

Immersion Evangelism

Any church that is not seriously involved in helping fulfill the Great Commission has forfeited its biblical right to exist.

—Oswald J. Smith

Jesus embedded Himself in His immediate world. He could be seen dining with a Pharisee and a tax collector one night then sitting around the campfire with a ruffian and a fisherman the next. Jesus did not avoid the controversial collision with society where religion and humanity often clash; on the contrary, He searched it out, attending weddings, funerals, banquets, and Jewish Sabbaths. After reading a discourse from Isaiah to a stunned crowd, he could walk from the synagogue and sit at a publican's house and expound on grace and mercy. One moment He could be seen in the courtyard of the temple, much to the Sadducees' surprise, and then moments later, He was at the side of the road with a beggar and blind man. The life of Jesus' ministry was one of complete immersion that contradicts most modern ministerial models and shatters our own preconceived ideologies. Jesus was the smell of fresh bread in a dank and dirty world. What are we?

There is a powerful picture of immersion in Matthew 5:2: "The people thronged Him." Jesus immersed Himself to the point where the masses pressed in around Him, hoping they could at least touch a thread of His clothes and be healed. Jesus did not seek some isolated place where a select number of people could have access to Him, but to the contrary, He literally immersed Himself and became a vivid picture of what the church should look like in our modern world: reachable, accessible, and the access point of healing and salvation.

This kind of lifestyle disqualified Jesus rather than garnered awards and invitations from the religious system of His day. He was not the popular conference speaker, and yet the sinners and dejected loved Him, clinging to every word, like drowning men. Today the Holy Spirit is seeking a multitude that will follow in Jesus' steps and immerse themselves into the culture of their day, the ebb and flow of life that rises and falls with every morning and evening. It looks like a wineskin turned inside out as the need for buildings and systematic Christianity gives way to outgoing public ministry. Our edifices and cultural icons that draw a stream of people every Sunday begin to be eclipsed by the light of our witness in the streets, parks, bus depots, skateboard parks, and every outdoor arena.

The only way we will ever come close to reaping this current harvest is when the church's conscience moves out from the fringes of the cities and immerses itself into the circulating heart of culture and life, inviting them into the Father's house. Can you imagine the day when "they bring forth the sick into the streets, laying them on beds and couches, that at least the shadow of Peter [the church] passing by might overshadow some of them" (Acts 5:15). That Acts church was so much a part of their culture and city that the streets became massive prayer lines and the open square, a healing room. The pool of Bethesda and its hard-to-reach waters gave way to a living, breathing church that saw people healed and set free wherever it traversed. Church was not quarantined to specific days of the week and difficult-to-find places, but rather there was a meeting on every corner and in every home. "And the Lord added to the church daily those who were being saved" (Acts 2:47).

The Acts church permeated every aspect of its society, and its message was unavoidable. No one had to search them out in some isolated commune as they commenced private worship. They were everywhere, as was the message of Jesus' death and resurrection. The church in Acts was so visible, immersed, and reachable that the city streets became the prayer line and Sabbath service. The shadow of revival was cast so large that no place was safe from its fire. They went from house to house and to the marketplace, and shouted from the rooftops a resurrected Jesus. "They were scattered abroad and went *everywhere* preaching the Word" (Acts 8:4, emphasis added). Do you see this picture of a revival-harvesting church? Such a church is completely immersed and active in the world around it to the point where every street and business is influenced and dramatically impacted by its presence.

What is our explanation? Are our cities and churches a bonfire of salvation inviting the sinner in? Or have we become so consumed with our own efforts and ambition for knowledge that we have disenfranchised ourselves from the least of our brethren, thus divorcing ourselves from Christ? The road to heaven is not paved with good intentions; it is, however, lined on the sidewalks with the hungry, thirsty, naked, imprisoned, and sick, who become the mile markers of our progress there.

And in the end, when we cross the finish line, we will hear those fateful words, "Inasmuch as you have done it unto one of the least of these My brethren, you have done it unto Me" (Matt. 25:40). Did you notice what He calls the prisoner, sick, hungry, and lost? "My brethren." Are they our brethren, or do we view them with critical disdain and smite our breast as the Pharisee and exclaim, "I thank you that I am not as other men are: extortionists, unjust, adulterers, or even as this publican. I fast twice a week and pay my tithes" (Luke 18:10–14). Who do you think goes home justified?

Are our cities resonating with truth and mercy, or are we still unwilling witnesses in the courts of God's grace? The two men on the road to Emmaus exclaimed, "Are you the only stranger in Jerusalem who has not known the things that have come to pass in these days?" (Luke 24:18). Our own neighborhoods, workplaces, schools, and streets need to be so saturated with His presence until they, too, shout, "Have you not known the things that have come to pass in these days?" It is not an easy road to find in this present maze of Christianity with its current trends and movements and all the prophetic fanfare. But it is possible if we renew our vows and return to our first love and review the contract that He drew out in His blood. "And he said to them all, 'If any man will come after Me, let him deny himself, and take up his cross daily, and follow Me'" (Luke 9:23).

Chapter 7

The Joy of Harvest

Someone asked, "Will the heathen who have never heard the gospel be saved?" It is more a question with me whether we—who have the gospel and fail to give it to those who have not—can be saved.
— Charles Spurgeon

Those who sow in tears shall reap in joy. "He who continually goes forth weeping, bearing seed for sowing, shall doubtless come again with rejoicing, bringing his sheaves with him" (Ps. 126:5–6).

It's difficult to explain to someone the inexpressible joy of harvest and what it does to the spirit, how it feels to know the suffering of the Lord and be an answer to countless tears and endless prayers resulting in the salvation of one soul. The countless tears are usually not your own, but you become a catalyst of another person's prayer as you share the good news of Jesus Christ.

There truly is no greater joy than the joy of harvest. Just look at heaven's response to this sowing in tears and reaping in joy. Only then will you begin to comprehend the extreme joy of harvest. "I say to you that likewise there will be *more joy* in heaven over one sinner who repents than over ninety-nine just persons who need no repentance" (Luke 15:7, emphasis added).

Heaven is a place where tears are nonexistent and the laborers receive their rewards, but stop for a moment and comprehend that there is more joy in heaven—more—for one sinner who repents than for all the trophies of the ninety-nine. You see, the joy of the Lord—read it again—the *joy of the Lord* is your strength. When you make Him happy, He makes you strong. Strength is often absent in many Christians' lives because they have not discovered what makes the Father happy. When one sinner repents, the elevator of eternity goes up and causes heaven to rejoice. This is the secret of your strength: reaping in joy!

Now wait—it doesn't end at the throne of God. That inexpressible joy of harvest doesn't stop with the Father; no, it echoes throughout the realms of heaven! "Likewise, I say to you, there is joy in the presence of the angels of God over one sinner who repents" (Luke 15:10). You see, all of heaven is in sync with the harvest of souls and is tuned into every crashing symbol and thundering drumbeat of it. Yet why, here on Earth, is it so misplaced and silenced? Do you desire to be in the *presence of the angels?* Then first be in the *presence of one sinner* who repents! That, according to Scripture, ushers in heaven to Earth and us into heaven more than any other dynamic. Read it again: "I say to you that likewise there will be *more joy* in heaven over one sinner who repents than over ninety-nine just persons who need no repentance." It's no surprise then that the great lover of God penned those words, "Those who sow in tears shall reap in joy."

When you make the painful sacrifice of self-will and take up your cross to follow Him, the result is irrefutably unspeakable joy. The reason the common atmosphere in many churches today is nominal and neutral at best is because there is no harvest! Even when joy is present, it seems short-lived; there is no doubt that the law of true sowing and reaping is not present there. You see, someone, somewhere, got the law of harvest mixed up and subjected it to the law of this present age, forgetting that godliness with contentment is great gain. The sowing and reaping God has intended that will secure the greatest joy and strength is the harvest of souls.

My friend, this is the riches "where neither moth nor rust destroys and where thieves do not break in and steal." (Matt. 6:20). The questions you have to ask yourself are, Am I making heaven rich? Is there more joy in heaven because of my hard work? The person who does not comprehend the joy of harvest now in this life will undoubtedly approach the gates of heaven a pauper. "So is he who lays up treasure for himself and is not rich toward God" (Luke 12:21).

C. H. Spurgeon, that great English evangelist, once said:

We will sigh and cry to God day and night until the blessing comes. This is the sowing, this is the ploughing, this is the harrowing—may it go on to harvesting. I long to hear my brethren and sisters universally saying, "We are full of anguish; we are in agony till souls be saved." The cry of Rachel, "Give me children, or I die," is the cry of your minister this day, and the longing of thousands more besides. As that desire grows in intensity, a revival is approaching. We must have spiritual children born to Christ, or our hearts will break for the longing that we have for their salvation. Oh, for more of these longings, yearnings, cravings, travailing! *If we plead till the harvest or revival comes, we shall partake in the joy of it (emphasis added).*

Once we get through the birth canal of weeping and travailing, we can then begin the song of joy because a son has been born. A soul has been born again, and new life has been added to heaven. In Jesus' closing moments on Earth, He taught this principle: "A woman, when she is in labor, has sorrow because her hour has come; but as soon as she has given birth to the child, she no longer remembers the anguish, for joy that a human being has been born into the world" (John 16:21).

Jesus Himself sowed in tears and reaped in the greatest joy. Remember the account of Paul: "Looking unto Jesus, the author and finisher of our faith, who for the joy that was set before Him endured the cross, despising the shame, and has sat down at the right hand of the throne of God" (Heb. 12:2). Will we endure our own cross and follow Him? Can we see past the shame of rejection and fear to the joy set before us? No one will experience true joy until he can embrace the sorrow of sowing and come to know the fellowship of His suffering. Like Hannah, we, too, will have our own bitterness of soul. But then we will have the great joy of harvest that will surely follow. Lord, let us follow You into the joy of harvest!

Chapter 8

Does the Church Really Want Revival?

"If Jesus had preached the same message that ministers preach today, He would never have been crucified."
— Leonard Ravenhill

The question this chapter poses is often a difficult one to answer and yet can quickly be gauged by a simple question. Do you have a tendency and desire to satisfy the needs of those saved and in attendance at your church, or are you equally and with the same intensity accommodating those outside of your regular Sunday attendance and special services? This is not a hard question to answer, but the answer may be uncomfortable to admit.

The amount of time it takes to keep people in church could win a city for Jesus if applied to those outside of it. Why are so many resources and so much energy expended to keep people in if being in was so appealing in the first place? God has put an invisible mechanism inside of every believer—*to go*. The more we attempt to restrain that internal drive of God's kingdom, the more we quench and kill the vision and calling until we are left with an impotent, power-less shell of what it was originally meant to be.

A Christian was never created to exist within the green-house-type environment that the normal church now promotes and propagates. This type of environment may allow a little sunlight to filter in, but it never really permits the church to become what it was meant to be, often because of fear of losing it. The contemporary church machine has mastered the art of mimicking liberty, but it's never really willing to throw down the walls of self-containment and self-preserva-tion and allow the blazing light of freedom to shine in. It wants to discuss revival but in the shadows silently protests any real change rather than risk the utter breakdown of its current structure.

Because so much of ourselves is built within it, the thought of how much of us would have to die is unbearable. So we continue the endless cycle of religious activity, recy-cling old ideas and redressing yesterday's revelation, hoping it will hold the attention of those listening from Sunday to Sunday. Revival has become a buzzword in a cartoon land-scape of modern Christianity where soft, well-intentioned men refuse to hazard their lives for Jesus Christ.

The residual flow of Christians continues to recirculate through conferences, repeating the same steps as before: prayer lines, personal prophecy, usually repeated or slightly rephrased revelation, then wash and do it again. What was always intended as equipping and releasing inevitably becomes old manna regurgitated and reinvented, resulting in a malnourished and emaciated body. We usually leave these meetings tired, drained, and powerless, and the commis-sion of Christ comes to a screeching halt, resulting in a vast population near and around these convocations that never hears or comprehends the saving message of salvation and transformation.

This phenomenon is not isolated to the American church, but we are definitely the parents of it. Other countries often resist this form of Christianity that Americans have packaged and produced at staggering speed. But, tragically, some do not and succumb to our habits, quickly becoming a mirror image of the suit-and-tie Western evangelist, adopting many of the same methods and divorcing themselves from New Testament power and succession.

There are rising numbers of Christians around the world, though, who are fleeing the Sunday morning institution and returning to a New Testament way of living. What they, too, must avoid is the same challenge that faces the former: Is the motivation stemming from an overwhelming desire to see the gospel preached to all the nations, or has it become another hybrid form of modern religion, different only in that it has less trappings and dress up? If the world around us is not our objective, then we become like Israel in the wilderness, continuing to wander without any real purpose except for being free from our previous captivity. This is the danger of many nontraditional movements today; they are going around the same mountain as others before them, but only in a different direction. What they will eventually become is just another group of Christians with a different set of values gathering in a slightly altered way.

Reaching the world and its evangelization have to be our objectives, as it was in the Acts church, or we will only become the very thing we fear: an institution. The original blueprint is easy to follow, and when married with present revelation, it will radically impact the world around us. The engine of self-preservation and its industrious counterpart, tradition, must be stalled by the fervent spirit of evangelism and revival that will keep a diligent watch against the subtle invasion of compromise.

Back to the question, Does the church as a whole really want revival? The answer in most cases is generally clear:

no! The easiest way to illustrate this is by our aggressive unwillingness to dispose of old wineskins and methods of assembly and function. We still honestly believe that the Sunday and Wednesday model, with its methodical, hypnotic drudgery, still reaches a new generation of truth-seekers. The normal Sunday morning slow dance with Jesus, followed by a systematic sermon, appeals to this generation like a Model-T Ford does to NASCAR; it doesn't fit and it's no longer relevant.

But the masses of all ages and religious backgrounds are suddenly waking up to the idea that the New Testament blueprint "met daily from house to house" and "added to the church daily those who were being saved." (Acts 2:47). The eye-opening revelation that church has nothing to do with a dark edifice with long unwelcoming pews is shocking, to say the least.

What was meant to be a pit stop for the revolution-aries and reformers to fuel up and set new fires quickly descended into a controlled, sterile environment where only the subjected and conformed could survive. But a new breed of passionate Christ-followers is springing upon the scene who will nail the DNA of revival to the old antique doors of modern institutionalism, like Martin Luther did in his day. The revolution has begun—are you its revolutionary?

Chapter 9

The Face of Revival

While women weep, as they do now, I'll fight; while children go hungry, as they do now, I'll fight; while men go to prison, in and out, in and out, as they do now, I'll fight; while there is a drunkard left, while there is a poor lost girl upon the streets, while there remains one dark soul without the light of God, I'll fight—I'll fight to the very end!

—William Booth

What does it look like? How can you look at any landscape and say, "That is revival"? Even the word *revival* has endured misunderstanding and abuse. But what is revival, and what does it look like? I have a clear definition for you: Harvest is the intuitive knowledge and insatiable hunger of a world to know God. *Revival is when God's people are overcome with the desire to see that hunger and knowledge available to every human being.* That's it. Read it again: *Revival is when God's people are overcome with the desire to see that hunger and knowledge available to every human being.*

The church revived is clearly a body that is consumed with the love of God and in that foundational passion lives and dies until a world that Jesus sacrificed Himself for is saved and born into His kingdom. If you peer through the curtains of history, this is the scarlet thread that is woven throughout it. Tragically, many claim to love God and have elaborate outward displays but are unwilling to reach beyond their own self-created boundaries and share what they have freely received. Can you imagine with me for one minute the church of Acts if it would have remained reclusive in the upper room after Pentecost?

The killer of most revivals defers to the modern modus operandi of most ministries: itineration. *Webster's* describes an itinerant minister as someone who "travels from place to place, especially on a circuit, as a minister, judge, or sales representative." As soon as we make the "sale" or collect our honorarium, we are out of town, despite the possibilities of revival in that region.

If you study the lives of revivalists throughout history, they often stayed months or even years in one region when visible signs of revival began. Today we are driven to succeed in ministry to such a degree that our personal gain and status among our peers have caused us to sacrifice the greater impact of a genuine move of God that can consume years and months of our lives. The future of revival lies at the feet of a generation that has counted the cost of personal gain and status quo, crashing the gates of modern ministry with a *cry of harvest.*

Again, *revival is when God's people are overcome with the desire to see that hunger and knowledge available to every human being.*

Revival has a face; it's humanity etched with the lines of necessity and pain, aching for reality and acceptance. It can be smudged black by coal from the mines of Pennsylvania or reddened by the rouge from a Las Vegas stage. But it has the same intent: salvation and the redeeming love of God.

The clarion call of John 3:16 is still the rudder of revival: "For God so loved the world that He gave His only begotten Son, that if anyone would believe in Him, he would not perish but have everlasting life." It is the gale wind that fills the sails of ministry, resulting in countless salvations and healing. It's the river that will reshape the church as we see it today washing away the debris of the past two hundred years.

Revival is imminent everywhere, and you can hear the sound of a rushing mighty wind in the rafters of today's church. There is hope, despite the bedrock of tradition; the wells are being dug again, releasing the ancient current of reformation that has left its mark from generation to generation. Once again a generation shall be *the face of revival.*

Chapter 10

Revival Praying

The church is looking for better methods; God is looking for better men. The Holy Ghost does not flow through methods, but through men. He does not come on machinery, but on men. He does not anoint plans, but men... men of prayer.

—E. M. Bounds

If there is any one ingredient in modern methodism that is clearly absent, it is the fire of revival praying. Oh, people pray every day: benedictions, earnest prayers over the Sunday offering, rapid-fire prayers over departing children as they race off to school, and a plethora of other meaningful, sincere prayers. But *revival praying* is a whole other dimension—lifestyle and passion. To revival pray means to cross the chasm of human affairs into the realm of Christ's intercession and stand in the gap. It is to be a bridge of justice and salvation to a world in unbelievable darkness and depravity; it is a road less traveled in a system of convenience and expediency.

First, let me tell you what revival praying is *not*. Revival praying is *not* the conveyor belt of Sunday morning where Christians find themselves in the gauntlet of prayer lines and prayer circles, ever praying for the same thing but never really coming to the place of complete breakthrough and broken-ness. Revival prayer is *not* the endless river of requests for financial blessings and a life less difficult, as everything we say, do, and pray defers inward.

Revival prayer is *not,* as some so adamantly conclude, endless adoration of a God who is not wrought with our own insecurities as we lose ourselves in what we call worship. As Abraham brought his only son, his life, his dreams, and his ambitions to the mountain with his knife, wood, and fire in hand, he went up to *worship* (Gen. 22:5)! Worship in Spirit and in truth, as the Lord still so adamantly seeks, is not selfish and self-satisfying, but rather selfless and sacrificial. That, my friend, is *revival praying.*

A perfect picture of revival praying that not only changes the inner man but also the perilous places present in the world around us in found in Acts 3. Peter and John's "hour of prayer" was not one of silent private petitions often found in the priestly duties or in the exclamatory prayers of the Pharisee who cried, "I fast twice in the week, and I give tithes of all that I possess" (Luke 18:12). But rather, the revival praying of Peter and John inevitably positioned them into the line of fire during their most hallowed devotion time. The ninth hour became the crossroads of power as the apostles' *revival praying* met the poor cripple's *revival crying,* resulting in unprecedented revival as he leaped and jumped in the temple square. The crippled man was revival's fuse; Peter and John were its match.

You see, we are not the only people praying for revival; the most earnest prayers for new life are coming, not from the church who has already found her physician, but from the destitute and dying who lie at the temple gate begging for alms. When those like Peter and John take themselves outside the comfortable catacombs of current devotion and place themselves in the crossfire of the desperate life-and-death crisis of the world around them, the result will be the reviving Spirit of Christ that raises the dead, heals the sick, and casts out their demons.

Where is your devotion, and to what end does it lead you? Are you really praying for revival, or is revival praying for you? Are you the catalyst of new life and power at the crossroads of human despair, or are you the rich ruler who passes by it every day? To really pray for revival, you must *be it* and cross the street of circumstance and stare it in the face.

Chapter 11

What Is My Reward Then?

*People who do not know the Lord ask why in the world
we waste our lives as missionaries. They forget that
they, too, are expending their lives.... and when the
bubble has burst, they will have nothing of eternal
significance to show for the years they have wasted.*
       —Nate Saint
       Missionary martyr

From the hallways of history, you can still hear the clarion
call of Paul: "What is my reward then? That when I
preach the gospel, I may present the gospel of Christ without
charge, that I may not abuse my authority in the gospel" (1
Cor. 9:18). Now we see a different bar raised with an outrageous price tag of $1,500, $3,000, or even $15,000. What is
your price? How much does it cost to buy you?

We sell tickets in our conferences for lunches and pastors'
meetings, all the while exiling a generation of true revivalists from the tables of compromise we have so lavishly
set. The banquet table that the Lord prepares seems much
different from our high-dollar buffets: "But when you give
a feast, invite the poor, the maimed, the lame and the blind"
(Luke 14:13–14). Once we empty the Gospel Mission shelter

and bus in the poor, we will begin to open the windows of heaven over our ministries. The only reason we have to work so hard to see any tangible results is because we have misappropriated the anointing. Get the sick who need a doctor into your midst; miracles will become humdrum rather than the calling card to charge high-dollar entry fees.

So the cycle of deception continues as the prophets demand a per diem for their free gifts and anointing that God has bestowed upon them, but could the greater sin be the masses of people who have come to purchase it? Yet the innocent spectators to this religious sporting event are the world and its masses; like in a great Roman amphitheatre, they watch us as we display our wares. They know the story of Jesus and how He was born of a virgin and died on the cross and was resurrected the third day. They have watched the movies and heard the stories, and they are not buying our contemporary version of Christianity anymore than they did in Peter's day or Micah's. The only ones we are fooling are ourselves.

I think Paul must have read Micah's retort to Israel centuries before: "Her heads judge for a bribe, her priests teach for pay, and her prophets divine for money. Yet they lean on the LORD, and say, 'Is not the LORD among us? No harm can come upon us'" (Mic. 3:11). But it doesn't stop there. The people have fallen into the trap set by modern ministries. They run from afar to pay these outrageous prices for something that Jesus purchased with His own blood so we could have it for free. They fill these conference lines by the tens of thousands and only reinforce a practice of deceit and greed.

Watch what Peter said to a man in his day who tried to pay for the gifts of the Holy Spirit: "And when Simon saw that through the laying on of the apostles' hands, the Holy Spirit was given, he offered them money, saying, 'Give me this power also, that anyone on whom I lay hands may receive the Holy Spirit.' But Peter said to him, 'Your money perish with you, *because you thought that the gift of God could be purchased with money!'* " (Acts 8:18–20, emphasis added). The stock market of modern ministry has high bidders and investors, but I dare say a crash is about to happen that will force us to refocus on the Great Commission.

Yet there is still an invitation to an abundant life: "Ho! Everyone who thirsts, come to the waters; and you who have no money, come, buy and eat. Yes, come, buy wine and milk without money and without price. *Why do you spend money for what is not bread, and your wages for what does not satisfy"* (Isa. 55:1–2, emphasis added). Did you get that? *"Why do you spend money for what is not bread, and your wages for what does not satisfy?"* We are taking our hard-earned wages and spending them on something that is free, and in the end, the parade of modern plagiarism does not satisfy us. We need to return to the unleavened bread of simplicity and truth and embrace the cadence of Christ passed down twenty centuries ago: "Heal the sick, cleanse the lepers, raise the dead, cast out devils: freely ye have received, freely give. Provide neither gold, nor silver, nor brass in your purses, nor scrip for your journey, neither two coats, neither shoes, nor yet staves: for the workman is worthy of his meat" (Matt. 10:8–10).

The pages of future revival will be a divine screenplay of eternal proportions as millions fill fields and open arenas, bringing with them a landslide of sin and decadence, only to be filled with supernatural power from on high and return to their cities and streets with a greater glory. Like Legion before them, they will be innumerable as they fill ballparks, movie theatres, soccer arenas, and the neon streets of such places as Las Vegas and Times Square.

As long as a price tag remains on any person of revival, it will only hinder and handicap what God desires to do. Paul declared, "For you are bought with a price" (1 Cor. 6:20). Every time we add to or take away from the great price Jesus paid, we demean and remove the great value that it demands. The great city-shakers of the future will walk with this blueprint in their soul: "I have raised him up in righteousness, and I will direct all his ways: *he shall build my city, and he shall let go my captives, neither for price nor reward, says the* LORD *of hosts"* (Isa. 45:13, emphasis added).

Chapter 12

The Gospel of Gain Has No Contentment

*Only as the church fulfills her missionary obligation
does she justify her existence.*
— Author unknown

There is no greater enemy to the harvest than the contemporary gospel of gain—the erroneous doctrine that preaches a message of self-absorption and endless wealth that will pave your road to heaven. It guarantees you a place in eternity and mountains of riches in this life as well.

This twenty-first-century doctrine dismisses the words of Christ and dresses Him up in fancy white suits and expensive baubles. If we superimposed the modern picture of Jesus that this present stable of preachers portrays over the biblical Christ who walked the earth two thousand years ago, what would it look like? Can you imagine a pampered, priestly figure prancing on the stages of Judea with a captivated audience as He exhorted them to give money in exchange for healing and salvation?

Wasn't this the same Jesus who said to the masses as they followed Him: "When you give a dinner or a supper, do not ask your friends, your brothers, your relatives, nor rich neighbors, lest they also invite you back, and you be repaid. But when you give a feast, invite the poor, the maimed, the lame, and the blind. And you will be blessed, because they cannot repay you; for you shall be repaid at the resurrection of the just" (Luke 14:12–14). A gospel that intends for the receiver to get richer and the poor to get poorer is a self-indulging one that contradicts the life and message of the one that they seemingly love and promote.

As Paul stated to Timothy, "But those who desire to be rich fall into temptation and a snare, and into many foolish and harmful lusts which drown men in destruction and perdition" (1 Tim. 6:9–10). When the desire to be rich is greater than the desire to see the lost found and those in despair saved, you have followed a gospel according to man. You have found yourself winding up a treacherous road with no end.

Armies of Christians waste years of their lives striving to get money in exchange for ministry. They say to themselves, "I am doing all of this to get the resources to go to the mission field and to fulfill my vision." But Jesus simply stated, "One thing you lack: Go your way, sell whatever you have and give to the poor, and you will have treasure in heaven; and come, take up the cross, and follow Me" (Mark 10:21). The deception that we must work exhaustively toward the goal of ministry is a false one, as millions of souls face a future without Christ as we reach for an elusive dream.

The words of James shatter this theory with startling severity:

> Look here, you people who say, "Today or tomorrow we are going to a certain town and will stay there a year. We will do business there and make a profit." How do you know what will happen tomorrow? For your life is like the morning fog—it's here a little

while, then it's gone. What you ought to say is, "If the Lord wants us to, we will live and do this or that." Otherwise you will be boasting about your own plans, and all such boasting is evil. Remember, it is sin to know what you ought to do and then not do it.

—James 4:13–17 NLT

The gospel of gain has no contentment as it relentlessly spins the wheels of personal achievement dressed up as an Easter Sunday Jesus who requires nothing more than a nominal commitment that never requires more than 10 percent. The cross of Jesus Christ has become a lottery ticket or a slot machine that promises you something greater than what you put into it willingly, forgetting that the cross demands sacrifice and death to self. Where in the world did we conjure up a doctrine that paints a picture of the cross as a place to get gain or glory? "Now godliness with contentment is great gain. For we brought nothing into this world, and it is certain we can carry nothing out" (1 Tim. 6:6–7).

We must get past this minefield of modern theology if we are ever going to effectively convert the nations to Jesus Christ. More potential missionaries, evangelists, and powerful ministries are sidelined because of these dangerous doctrines leaving millions cheering from the pews of modern church as the world remains dark and divided. The only answer may be an Elijah-type experience where the fire of God begins to burn up these man-made altars and send us back to the front lines where He always intended us to be.

The prodigal son of our generation is not a drunken, backslidden one, but rather a lukewarm, nominally committed one who is relaxed and retired as the end of the age looms on the horizon. I make this challenge to all of you who fall into this category to "stir thyself up" and find your place in the trenches again! What nation or culture draws your heart and digs up the dead old cisterns of vision in your heart? To that end, then, you must move with all your heart, even if it means the loss of all that you might have gained in your religious retirement. It is time to possess your land!

"Ask of me, and I shall give thee the heathen for your inheritance, and the uttermost parts of the earth for thy possession" (Psalm 2:8) was David's prayer. What is yours? Are you asking God for more than just your own security and your family's future? Can you see past your daughter's or son's college graduation, or have you become so rooted and grounded in this present life that you are no longer any heavenly good? Does the plight of nations, ghettos, and the widespread plague of poverty move you anymore? Have you forgotten what it feels like or what Jeremiah must have felt when he cried out with tears: "Oh, my anguish, my anguish! I writhe in pain. Oh, the agony of my heart! My heart pounds within me, I cannot keep silent. For I have heard the sound of the trumpet; I have heard the battle cry" (Jer. 4:19).

Chapter 13

The Curse of Canaan

The true greatness of any church is not how many it seats, but how many it sends!
—Author unknown

"Cursed be Canaan; a servant of servants he shall be to his brethren" (Gen. 9:25). The story is found in Genesis 9. It tells of a moment in Noah's life when he was vulnerable and naked: "And Noah began to be a farmer, and he planted a vineyard. Then he drank of the wine and was drunk, and became uncovered in his tent" (vv. 20–21).

Many times the Lord will allow us to be "uncovered" before those around us, not to reveal our nakedness and need for covering, but rather to reveal the motives and intents of the hearts of those looking from the outside in. Watch the younger son's reaction to his father's obvious nakedness and vulnerability: "And Ham, the father of Canaan, saw the nakedness of his father, and told his two brothers outside" (v. 22). Ham's tragic mistake was that he revealed and exploited his father's moment of weakness and nakedness. Whatever his motive, it brought down a curse that is still alive and active in the body of Christ.

Look at the two elder brothers' reaction to Ham's revelation: "But Shem and Japheth took a garment, laid it on both their shoulders, and went backward and covered the nakedness of their father. Their faces were turned away, and they did not see their father's nakedness" (v. 23). The garment they took to cover their father is symbolic today of the blood of Jesus. Their faces were turned away; they wouldn't even allow themselves to see their father's nakedness.

Now watch what happened when Noah awoke from his stupor: "So Noah awoke from his wine, and knew what his younger son had done to him. Then he said, 'Cursed be Canaan; a servant of servants he shall be to his brethren'" (vv. 24–25). We are still abiding under Canaan's curse today. When we run to reveal our brother's and sister's nakedness and obvious vulnerability, we ignorantly and, even willingly at times, bring down this curse upon our household—the curse of Canaan.

Now look at the second part of this curse: "A servant of servants he shall be to his brethren." The church has become, by and large, a slave to a system bound by laws and traditions and archaic formulas and rituals. Instead of a body where every part has equality, we have become a ruling faction where the stronger rule over the weaker; we have become slaves to one another.

Jesus, however, taught us just the opposite: "But Jesus called them to Himself and said, 'You know that the rulers of the Gentiles lord it over them, and those who are great exercise authority over them. Yet it shall not be so among you; but whoever desires to become great among you, let him be your servant'" (Matt. 20:25–26). But the curse of Canaan has created an opposite force at work among us. The root of it is our exposing and exploiting of one another. Yet the greatest tragedy in this whole scenario is that the world sees right through it, and eventually a harvest is lost.

What we so desperately need right now is the blessing of Shem and Japheth: "And he said: 'Blessed be the LORD, the God of Shem, and may Canaan be his servant. May God enlarge Japheth, and may he dwell in the tents of Shem; and may Canaan be his servant" (vv. 26–27). The major reason we have not been "enlarged" and come to fruition in our visions and desires is because we have walked in the footsteps of Ham and exposed and exploited one another in the body of Christ. We have become like the mob that dragged the adulteress woman to Jesus and cast her at His feet, demanding judgment and justice. Jesus did give them His justice, though — His mercy.

Until we are able to stoop in the dirt with the downcast and broken, with our brothers and sisters, we will never look revival eye to eye. We will continue to skirt around true transformation, entertaining one another from meeting to meeting, and all the while the world perishes around us. We must break this curse of Canaan at all cost, in Jesus' name. The only way to do this is to react in the opposite spirit that Ham did. We must become Shems and Japheths and cover one another. In doing this, the curse can be reversed.

The word *covered* in Hebrew is *kawsaw,* which literally means to "fill up hollows"; by implication it means "to cover (for clothing or secrecy)"; "clothe, conceal, cover (self), or hide." This is exactly what Shem and Japheth did to their father in his nakedness; they concealed him, hid him, and literally clothed him. We find the same principle in the New Testament: "And above all things have fervent love for one another, for love will cover a multitude of sins" (1 Pet. 4:8). Does this justify my sin or anyone else's sin? God forbid. But our reaction to one another is critical.

The world watched the spectacle of the church and her reaction to Jim Bakker, and they screamed, they cried, and they died. Every time we react outside of the context of God's love, the curse of Canaan extends its borders to encompass more of this generation. We need to cry out above all for *wisdom* in this hour. We need to cling to the wisdom of the Lord as the battle intensifies. We need to put out the fires of gossip and slander, not add wood to them with our words and accusations. "Where there is no wood, the fire goes out; and where there is no talebearer, strife ceases" (Prov. 26:20).

Lord, give us Your heart in this hour. As the greatest harvest in Earth's history dawns upon us, give us the wisdom of Solomon, the heart of David, and the prayer of Paul: "Love suffers long and is kind; love does not envy; love does not parade itself, is not puffed up; does not behave rudely, does not seek its own, is not provoked, thinks no evil; does not rejoice in iniquity, but rejoices in the truth; bears all things, believes all things, hopes all things, endures all things. Love never fails" (1 Cor. 13:4–8). Then and only then will the world know that we are Christians—by the love we have for one another.

Chapter 14

Open Heavens and Extreme Harvest

I have but one passion: It is He, it is He alone. The world is the field and the field is the world; and henceforth that country shall be my home where I can be most used in winning souls for Christ.
— Count Nicolaus Ludwig von Zinzendorf

Let me explain the title of this chapter, "Open Heavens and Extreme Harvest." I had one of the most unusual and powerful experiences of my life recently. I was a speaker at a conference in Orlando, Florida, called, "Let the Prophet Speak." It was a different landscape, as the church was predominantly African-American, and many of the speakers were not familiar to me, with the exception of Bishop Bill Hamon. That night the sanctuary was nearly filled as approximately four hundred people came to hear the word from Bishop Hamon, whom many consider as the pioneer of the current prophetic movement. As Bill spoke, there was a brief interruption followed by an announcement that the pastor's wife had had a heart attack and was being rushed to the hospital. This prompted fervent prayer as the meeting continued.

Sometime later the entire atmosphere suddenly changed as the announcement swept the sanctuary that the pastor's wife had passed from this world and entered eternity. The place exploded as people began to cry out to God in an unprecedented way. The sound that emanated from that church was not of this world, friend, as heaven and Earth suddenly collided. The Scripture, "And from the days of John the Baptist until now, the kingdom of heaven suffereth violence, and the violent take it by force," suddenly took on a life of its own. Four hundred people began to cry out to God in one accord. Copastor and First Lady of this church was pronounced dead at 9:32 P.M. on Thursday, June 29, 2006. I was scheduled to speak the following morning and evening.

When I entered the sanctuary to minister on the next day, only hours later, the atmosphere had clearly changed. There was an expectancy that did not exist before. Everyone knew something very unique had to be taking place for such unusual and unexpected events to be transpiring. I was honestly at a loss as to what to say until I took the microphone during worship that morning and evening and the prophetic word was declared with force and clarity, both personally and by many in attendance. This is some of what unfolded.

"The death of one thing will bring to life something else" became the clarion call of the evening as this prophetic song progressed:

The Lord says that from this seed, a million souls will be reaped in Orlando! A million souls will come into the kingdom as a result of this one seed. For the Lord declares over you an open heaven and an extreme harvest! The Lord says a new precedent is now set over Florida and this nation, and the heavens will be opened as My people contend in this way. For I am releasing my angels of vindication, restitution, and harvest as the reaper overtakes the sower.

As Enoch went up into heaven and never returned to Earth but stood in the gap and kept the door in heaven opened, even as Elijah went up and never returned to Earth—he also kept the heavens open— and a double portion was given to that nation, so now she is standing in the gap and an open heaven is available to us here, right now!

Many more words in this context were released that morning and evening. I truly believe that all across this country and the world, we can take hold of this open heaven with them in Orlando, Florida. In *extreme harvest,* traumatic and violent things often will occur that will create a "suddenly," as it did in Acts 2 on the day of Pentecost. Did you ever ask yourself why thousands were saved after the death and resurrection of Jesus on the day of Pentecost? The violent, tumultuous times produced an *extreme harvest.*

The reason we are experiencing record-breaking floods, hurricanes, earthquakes, and other natural disasters is because we are in a time of *extreme harvest.* This only underwrites the dire need for all of us to position ourselves in every general meeting we assemble in to take this harvest by force. We cannot afford to lose one second of what has been spent to secure this open heaven. It is commonly reported that there are open heavens in certain regions, cities, and, more often, at conferences. But you must ask yourself, "Is this open heaven we are declaring resulting in an extreme harvest?" If not, then it stands to question if there is really an open heaven at all.

The problem can be twofold: (1) There really isn't an open heaven, or (2) we have simply not responded to the opportunity of extreme harvest that this open heaven creates.

The latter is often true; we simply take this open heaven for granted and move on to something more experiential or self-satisfying and never seize and reap this harvest springing up all around us. Jeremiah had a similar experience when he prophesied, "The harvest is past, the summer is ended, and we are not saved" (Jer. 8:20). The season of extreme harvest in Jeremiah's era went unattended and unnoticed, thus ending in disaster and loss.

I want to show you a progression, or evolution, in context to open heavens and extreme harvest as described above. First, we see Enoch, who got caught up into heaven and disappeared, never to be seen again. There is something about Enoch, though, that must be pointed out. Enoch represented one of the first prophetic dispensations upon the earth. Jude testifies about Enoch: "the seventh from Adam, prophesied of these, saying, Behold, the Lord cometh with ten thousands of his saints" (Jude 14).

See, Enoch was a "heaven opener" and prophesied the future and what must certainly come to pass. Likewise did Elijah. Elijah, too, was a heaven opener. "Elijah was a man subject to like passions as we are, and he prayed earnestly that it might not rain: and it rained not on the earth by the space of three years and six months. And he prayed again, and the heaven gave rain, and the earth brought forth her fruit" (James 5:17–18). You see, we all can be heaven openers, but are we willing to pay the price to do so and become extreme harvesters?

"And it came to pass, as they still went on, and talked, that, behold, there appeared a chariot of fire, and horses of fire, and parted them both asunder; and Elijah went up by a whirlwind into heaven" (2 Kings 2:11). This open heaven created a double portion of anointing, and Elisha, who inherited it, seized the moment and later declared an *extreme harvest!* "Then Elisha said, Hear ye the word of the LORD; thus saith the LORD, Tomorrow about this time shall a measure of fine flour be sold for a shekel, and two measures of barley for a shekel, in the gate of Samaria" (2 Kings 7:1). You see, we cannot have open heavens without extreme harvest! But we must also discern this and begin to declare it over our cities, churches, and nation and then be willing and ready to step out and possess it, as Elisha did. Remember, open heavens inevitably produce opportunities for extreme harvest. You can either stand in the prayer line and receive your open heaven or press on further into a double portion resulting in *open heavens and extreme harvest,* as Elisha did.

Paul was also a heaven opener and an extreme harvester; he went up into heaven but came back down to Earth to reap it! "And I knew such a man, (whether in the body, or out of the body, I cannot tell: God knoweth;) how that he was caught up into paradise, and heard unspeakable words, which it is not lawful for a man to utter" (2 Cor. 12:3–4).

I believe the kingdom evolution that is taking place is that we can now go up into the heavens, opening doors over cites and regions, and then come back down and, unlike Paul, who was limited in his dispensation, begin to *declare what we have seen and heard.* This will produce harvest unlike anything the earth has ever witnessed or seen before. We will bring down strongholds, but then we will seize the open heavens with great force and tenacity to reap tens and hundreds of thousands, even millions, into the kingdom of God. This open heaven that we will secure will be an eternal vacuum of heavenly advantage that will sweep them into the kingdom of God, unparalleled in human spiritual experience. Are you ready?

Chapter 15

Winning the World One City at a Time

If missions languish, it is because the whole life of godliness is feeble. The command to go everywhere and preach to everybody is not obeyed until the will is lost by self-surrender in the will of God. Living, praying, giving, and going will always be found together.

— Arthur T. Pierson

In three years, Jesus unfurled the DNA of ministry past, present, and future. The entire blueprint is captured in those brief three years. The spectrum of ministry is framed in Matthew, Mark, Luke, and John. Peek through the portal of the words written in red and you will find the foundation of every ministry that has ever truly existed or is yet to exist. Once you establish that fact in your spirit, then you begin to envision the call of God on your life and its deep, eternal ramifications on planet Earth.

Winning the world for Jesus has been one of the most dialogued, written about, and debated subjects in history, and it continues to mystify the masses. This single subject alone generates more books and essays than possibly any other topic. Yet when you peel back the layers of modern theology, the blueprint of ministry stands out blazingly clear, like an ancient treasure map waiting to be discovered. You suddenly realize the eternal plan of the ages: win the world *one city at a time.*

As Jesus emerged from the desert overcoming the temptations of the devil, He stepped into the shadowed edifice of the temple and opened Isaiah 61 and read out loud to the stunned audience: "The Spirit of the Lord God is upon me; because the LORD hath anointed me to preach good tidings unto the meek; he hath sent me to bind up the brokenhearted, to proclaim liberty to the captives, and the opening of the prison to them that are bound." (Luke 4:18).

On that fateful day, the public ministry of Jesus began. It wasn't met with high-profile endorsements, book reviews, or fanfare; but to the contrary, Jesus faced the sharp brow of the city, and the course of His ministry was set as he looked down at the rocks below. Later in this same chapter, a very revealing statement is made by the Lord, which is the first clue on the road to ministry: "And he said unto them, I must preach the kingdom of God to other cities also: for therefore am I sent" (Luke 4:43).

In that one brief moment in time, the strategy for world missions and evangelism was revealed to millions who would someday follow in His footsteps: "I must preach the kingdom of God to other cities also." The pressing, unshakable gravity of the kingdom compelled Jesus forward into new regions and cities to propagate heavenly seeds that would someday grow into historic revivals. This mandate for ministry is still the standard today. *We can win the world one city at a time!*

Fast forward with me, if you will, to another red-letter text in Acts 1, and again you will see Jesus casting the plumb line for world evangelization: "But you shall receive power when the Holy Spirit has come upon you; and you shall be witnesses to Me in Jerusalem, and in all Judea and Samaria, and to the ends of the earth" (Acts 1:8).

Once the Holy Spirit came upon them, just as it did Jesus in the muddy waters of the Jordan, it would be the compass of world harvest and missions—*one city at a time*. From what Jesus is stating, we can conclude that cities are the keys that open the doors to nations and worldwide revival. As we target the cities of the earth, both small and large, we begin to topple the network of darkness that holds a monopoly in these metropolitan centers.

These concrete and man-made epicenters become the radiuses by which the Holy Spirit moves and transforms the world. Minister, we must begin to concentrate our efforts in our cites or risk again that world harvest will hide from this generation as it has those before it. Jeremiah prophesied that tragic end to a church era when he prophesied, "The harvest is past, the summer is ended, and we are not saved" (Jer. 8:20).

The church must come out of the contemporary mind-set that abandons the streets and infrastructures of its cities and begin to invade them with every form of ministry and creativity at its disposal. Once we begin to open this ancient strategy that Jesus first laid out, we will see the heavens open and entire cities filled with joy, as Philip did. This is the "treasure" that Isaiah described, that was "out of darkness" and within reach of every believer. (Isaiah 45:3).

Let's fast forward again and see this same divine strategy at work one more time. Philip must have taken a page from His master's playbook as he went down to Samaria despite the current conditions or trends of the church. Rather than setting up a tent *outside* Samaria, Philip dove directly into the line of fire and hit the bull's-eye. He didn't dodge the fiery darts of the enemy; he went headlong toward them and dared the powers that be to confront him. Philip went to downtown Samaria and set up camp.

If we would simply apply this profound principle discovered in Acts 8, we would see harvest exponentially progressed in every city of the world. Rather than expecting the world to meander into our meetings one by one, we would put every convocation we conscripted into the direct line of fire and within yards of the city streets, gambling casinos, red-light districts, rent halls, theatres, arenas, and other downtown venues, and unleash the glory of God we are so fond of fostering and talking about. Let the glory finally do what it was always created to do: *win the world to Jesus.*

Chapter 16

Taking the City: The Gideon Upgrade

This generation of Christians is responsible for this generation of souls on the earth!
                                        —Keith Green

Gideon received a heavenly upgrade when God gave him the strategy to win the battle despite the incredible odds that were invariably stacked against them. "And the Lord said to him, Surely I will be with you and you shall defeat the Midianites *as one man.*" (Judges 6:16). The same effort, energy, and strength that it would take to defeat one man were now applied to thousands. This puts into perspective what the Lord must have meant when He stated, "How should one chase a thousand, and two put ten thousand to flight?" (Deut. 32:30).

Suddenly the Lord had downgraded tens of thousands of Midianites and Amalekites into the equivalent of one man. The same capacity to prophesy, preach, and bring to salvation one individual is transformed in the anointing to reach millions. This quantum leap of anointing suddenly puts world harvest into the crosshairs of our vision. It's no longer an impossible leap across a chasm of statistics, but rather a tangible reality to the ones who will believe it. God can give you a nation or a city, as He did Gideon, if you can climb the walls of rationale and believe His Word.

This divine dynamic is seen throughout the Scriptures as God takes mere humans and clothes them with power to take on insurmountable odds and numbers. Listen to the amazing promise found in Leviticus: "And five of you shall chase an hundred, and an hundred of you shall put ten thousand to flight" (Lev. 26:8). David and his mighty men experienced this, and Samson did as well. We see this supernatural anointing translated into the New Testament as Philip stared down the barrel of witchcraft and sorcery while an entire city was gripped by its evil. Suddenly the tables were turned, and the entire city was filled with joy as they *saw* and *heard* the miracles that Philip did! God amplified the efforts of one man, and it became like dynamite that blew open the doors of the city.

The only factors that are separating us from these kinds of results are our obedience and understanding. Are we willing to step out of the boat of contemporary methods and expect a city to be saved? Why did they get these kinds of results in their spiritual infancy and yet in all our acceleration and revelation, we see considerably less? The answer is simple: we need to desire and depend on it as intensely as they did. They had one consuming desire, and it was the same desire that moved Christ. As soon as you can break the gravity of this present Christian experience and accept the fact you are called to win the world to Jesus—despite the fact that you are only one person—the results will be phenomenal. You will receive the "Gideon upgrade," and your city and nation will be "as one man."

Jesus was a city-taker too. "And he said unto them, I must preach the kingdom of God to other cities also: for therefore am I sent" (Luke 4:43). Did you see that? Jesus literally defined His ministry in one broad stroke: "I must preach the kingdom of God to other cities also: for this reason I am sent." Jesus was born to take cities for the kingdom of God, and so are you.

Why are you sent? What is your duty? What is your calling? Whether from your back porch or the school yard, you are called to impact your city. It is yours through Christ; His calling continues seamlessly through you today. Step out and take it.

Chapter 17

Operation Harvest: God's Special Forces

Special operations are forces that fight unconventional battles that ordinary line infantry is incapable of. It requires a special type of warrior.

— www.specwar.net

Gideon was Special Forces. David was Special Forces. Moses and Aaron were Special Forces. Each of these biblical warriors engaged the enemy in an unconventional manner. Gideon's army was massively outnumbered and outgunned, yet prevailed. David refused the proven weapons of battle and chose his own. Moses and Aaron were on a special ops assignment that took them deep into enemy territory. Their mission in military terms was an "extraction" because the people of Israel were POWs (prisoners of war).

We have many today who have been captured by the enemy and held prisoner on the streets and in the bars, taverns, prison houses, and jails. Isaiah saw this challenge: "But this is a people robbed and spoiled; they are all of them snared in holes, and they are hid in prison houses: they are for a prey, and none delivers; for a spoil, and none says, 'Restore!' " (Isa. 42:22).

The Lord is again raising up Special Forces who will invade and extract His MIAs (missing in action) and POWs. They will be ready and radically different from the status quo in present soft-spun Christianity. Most will be unaccepted in the contemporary army, yet are highly qualified to fulfill the mission the Lord has for them.

David's mighty men were a Special Forces prototype. They were not fit for King Saul's army, although their apparent skill in battle and unique abilities qualified them for David's regiment. There résumés read something like this: "And every one that was in distress, and every one that was in debt, and every one that was discontented, gathered themselves to him; and he became a captain over them: and there were with him about four hundred men" (1 Sam. 22:2). Not your typical spreadsheet for ministry these days, is it?

These spiritual Special Forces are being raised up today for a highly critical assignment: *Operation Harvest*. God is sending them deep into enemy territory; they are His special ops, men and women who "endure hardness, as a good soldier of Jesus Christ" (2 Tim. 2:3). They have been intensely trained for years for this exact moment in history by the hard, extracting tests of life. Most of them will never be recognized or even remembered in this current life except by the ones rescued, but their heroics and actions will set the stage for the coming of Christ. Their objective is simply this: "This gospel of the kingdom shall be preached in all the world for a witness to all nations; and then shall the end come" (Matt. 24:14).

These end-time Special Forces have been raised up to combat the evolved tactics and strategies of the enemy. They do not use proven methods or contemporary strategies to tear down these spiritual strongholds that hold captive entire nations. Their methods will be questioned, scrutinized, and even despised by the rest of the army, but the end result will be irrevocable. These Special Forces know their objective and will achieve it no matter the cost. They are even now being recruited from churches, ministries, streets, prisons, brothels, and every other dark corner of existence. Their life experiences and conquering spirits have qualified them. Like Jonah, they will be ejected back onto the shores of the original mission: *Operation Harvest.*

"The SFOD-Delta unit was created in secrecy. The Delta was intended as an overseas counterterrorist unit specialized in hostage rescue, barricade operations, and specialized reconnaissance. The composition and strength of Delta Force are closely guarded secrets. Delta Force's main function is as a hostages' rescue unit. The recruits for Delta Force are volunteers mainly from the Eighty-second Airborne, Special Force Green Berets, and the Rangers. They are trained in all aspects of counterterrorism, and they are said to be the world's best specialists in CQB (close quarters battle)." (www.specwar.net)

Even in the natural, we are facing an extreme change in our approach to war. This radical change in modern-day warfare has demanded a change in its warriors and their training. Delta Force is the epitome of this change. They are a clandestine group of highly skilled soldiers whose primary purpose is to combat terrorism and facilitate hostage rescue. If we are to face this new threat of the enemy posing as a follower of Christ, we must begin to train our students differently as well.

Many of the old methods of evangelism, church planting, and training are no longer effective. Our inner cities and marketplaces demand a much different breed of warrior that can adapt instantly to his or her surroundings, melting into the enemy's camp, even as the spies did in Joshua, utilizing tactics and strategies that have never been attempted before.

These new strategies will literally topple regional and national strongholds and liberate entire cities.

Philip was Delta Force. In the book of Acts, chapter 8, Philip broke away from conventional thinking and methods and applied a strategy never seen before: he went down to Samaria. Samaria was the seat of the enemy's power and presence in the region and was untouched by that present revival. This one lone warrior engaged the principalities and powers over the region, and an entire city was liberated from captivity—counterterrorist and hostage rescue.

This new breed of soldier will not fear the awesome odds against them. They will see the objective and apprehend it. They will defy contemporary thinking and traditional methods that would never allow such radical maneuvers. They will take cities and the result will be clear: "There was great joy in that city" (Acts 8:8).

We are in the midst of a spiritual "draft." The time to be recruited, when the choice of service was up to us, is over. God is drafting his end-time warriors as He did in the book of Joel: "Proclaim ye this among the Gentiles; prepare for war, wake up the mighty men, let all the men of war draw near; let them come up" (Joel 3:9).

There is a "coming up" occurring in the kingdom of God. Many in the backdrop of modern Christianity are being called to the front lines, rising in spiritual rank and authority, sometimes overnight. God is waking up His mighty ones. They cannot slumber to the hypnotic tones of religion any longer; a massive equipping is under way. The officers are passing through the camp crying, "Prepare!" (Josh. 1:11).

The first draft in America occurred during the Civil War. Freedom from slavery was the cry then, and freedom from spiritual slavery is the cry now. God is setting the captives free within the confines of religion and the world. We are facing an epic Civil War again as the battle lines are drawn in the shifting sands of an ever-changing landscape. Which side will we be found standing on: freedom or slavery?

The Lord will begin to determine for many which side they are on. Are they freedom fighters fighting for the freedom of their cities and streets, or are they reinforcing the slavery and bondage that grip the heart of our land? If we stay neutral and do nothing, then we are enslaved ourselves and in need of recovery. We must begin to march forward and repossess the land.

"Regardless of their military or psychological effect, Special Forces units require more support than conventional units. Because they are traveling in smaller teams, they require air support to survive if caught by a larger unit they can't break free from. Some missions require extra planning and intelligence. The higher state of readiness these units possess call for an aggressive training regiment that is naturally more expensive than a peacetime infantry battalion." (www.specwar.net)

Air support, or strategic intercession, will be imperative, however, to the Special Forces' success. This was a key in the unsuccessful Delta Force mission in Mogadishu, Somalia, on October 3, 1993. They assaulted different safe houses containing high-ranking members of warring clans and took them prisoner. Unfortunately, during their last mission, two of the support helicopters from the 160th SOAR were shot down. Two Delta operators were killed defending the survivors of the second crash, and at least one was killed in an on-foot extraction through a city populated with locals riled up against the Americans. Air support is critical to the success or failure of each mission.

"But they that wait upon the LORD shall renew their strength; they shall mount up with wings as eagles" (Isa. 40:31). Intercession will be the wings of God's Special Forces. It will enable them to go into places previously impenetrable and deposit His liberating power. God's Delta

Force is even now being equipped and deployed for special service and missionary endeavors. A new approach in training is inevitable if we are ever going to see mass success. If we are ever going to really win the battles that confront us on the changing battlefields, we must allow for this new breed to emerge. They are in the cave of Adullam, training, preparing, and receiving new orders from the kingdom of God. They are even now in a preparatory position to launch out into strategic places around the globe to fulfill this great campaign: *Operation Harvest.*

Chapter 18

Reconnoiter: The Act of War

To examine, as the surrounding country, especially before making a military movement.
— Definition of *reconnoiter*

The armies of Israel had gathered en masse at the Jordan River. They began by deploying twelve spies to the land of Canaan. Moses commanded the scouts to take to the high ground and spy out the land. For forty days, they reconnoitered and gathered information to report back to headquarters so that a strategy could be formulated and the armies of Israel deployed. But to Israel's dismay, ten of the twelve spies brought back an evil report: "We are not able to go up against this people, for they are stronger than we.... They are giants and we are but mere grasshoppers in comparison" (Num. 13:31–33).

Instead of gathering the information they were ordered to attain, they returned in fear, assailing God's people with reports of defeat. Fear began to race through the camp, which inevitably resulted in retreat. Suddenly they forgot the mighty miracles that had gotten them to this point and gave in to trepidation and fear.

In this hour, the Lord is positioning His army for offensive maneuvers and strikes and to aggressively begin to strategize and occupy new terrain. Perfect love is driving out fear, and we are beginning to reach out beyond the perimeters and boundaries of the wilderness of today's landscape and possess the land. The spies are now returning from the concrete jungles of modern cities, not with reports of giants, but with reports of victory, strategy, and exploits.

The presence of the Lord is beginning to appear in the midst of us like never before. His glory is being manifested, not for us to revel and relish in, but, to the contrary, to empower and embolden us to cross over the Jordan and possess the land He has granted to us. This is a time for offensive strikes, not defensive parlays! This is the hour to launch out into the deep and begin to net a great catch. We cannot remain in the shallow, hallowed church buildings but must go out into the streets and public places. The cry is going through the camp, "Prepare! For in three days, we will cross over this Jordan." (Joshua 1:11).

Harvest is defined in *Webster's Dictionary,* not only as "to reap and gather," but also as, "to win, as a reward or gain from service." Harvest is not only a season of increase and abundance; it's also a time of conquest and overcoming, advancement and warfare, coupled with strategic militant maneuvers that advance the kingdom of God in secular society. Harvest is not the sound of retreat, but rather the trumpet call to arms employing our greatest forces and tactics to set the captives free.

Paul must have understood this militant mind-set when he wrote these memorable words: "No man that goes to war entangles himself with civilian affairs, that he may please him who has chosen him to be a soldier" (2 Tim. 2:4). A militant mentality is coming upon the church so that she may advance with tactical supremacy and take back land surrendered in fear and spiritual ignorance. God is enlisting soldiers who will obey orders from heaven and take critical ground, releasing prisoners of war who have been taken captive by the enemy. The lost are God's POWs and MIAs, and we are His front line.

Let's look at a historic battlefield for a moment. From July 1 to July 3, 1863, in the fields and woods just outside the small town of Gettysburg, Pennsylvania, a historic battle took place that would be considered the turning point of the Civil War. Over ninety-seven thousand Union troops set out to stop a full-force northern invasion of the Confederate army. As July 2, 1863, dawned, high ground called Little Round Top was unoccupied by either side. But both commanders clearly saw the possibilities there. Union commander General George Meade saw the need to defend the big hills in the south "round tops," while his adversary, General Robert E. Lee, saw those same hills as an opportunity to outflank Meade's troops and get behind them. The Confederates came up just a bit short, with their vanguard stopped by a single Union regiment in the woods below Little Round Top.

The battle of Gettysburg was a decisive engagement in that it arrested the Confederates' second and last major invasion of the North, destroyed their offensive strategy, and forced them to fight a defensive war. Once the high ground was taken, the battle that seemingly had been swaying towards the South was drastically changed. At this important junction, the war was won. Though the battles raged on for nearly another year, this blow and victory decided the future of both armies and the immediate future of a nation. During the three days of battle, the Union army had approximately twenty-three thousand casualties, and the Confederates had at least twenty-five thousand. At the high ground, destiny was decided, and so it is in the spiritual realm as well. Prayer fortifies us, and strategic evangelism advances the army.

Recently a friend and I stood on this very battleground in Gettysburg, Pennsylvania. As I walked through the rock defenses and bulwarks hastily made at night by the Union soldiers as they dug in to protect the high ground on Little Round Top, I was overwhelmed with a sense of urgency for the church to begin to occupy the high ground in the spiritual realm and not give another inch of soil to the enemy. So many neighborhoods, streets, businesses, and cities have been surrendered to the enemy without as much as a fight.

Before Gideon engaged the enemy, he took the high ground. Moses stood on the high mountain overlooking the battle, and as long as he maintained that position, Israel prevailed. We need to get a strategy from heaven for our own cities and begin to march their streets in prayer, intercession, and creative evangelism, implementing the tools and weapons God is entrusting to us in this current harvest.

Gettysburg was won by the resolve and determination of one regiment of soldiers who refused to give the enemy ground. If they would have given an inch, Confederate forces would have flanked the Union army and defeat would have been imminent for the North. Because of the courage and fortitude of the Union soldiers, however, the North won the Civil War, as well as freedom for millions of enslaved people. Harvest is "to win, as a reward or gain from service."

Paul instructed Timothy, "This charge I commit to you, son Timothy, according to the prophecies that were spoken over you, that you might wage a good warfare" (1 Tim. 1:18). It was the prophetic word spoken over him and through him that would determine the outcome of the battles that lay ahead. Paul exhorted Timothy to use this secret weapon to wage war on the enemy.

Ezekiel also implemented this strategy over the slain army of Israel. He prophesied to the dry bones and they lived! When we begin to prophesy the destiny and purposes of God over our neighborhoods and cities, we will begin to see the battle turn, even as they did in Gettysburg. As we begin to possess the high places in prayer and invade the dark areas of our cities and prophesy, we will experience the same results of revival and reformation that others have.

Like Gideon we cannot ignore the idolatry and new-age strongholds any longer. We must purpose our efforts toward these areas and intercede and prophesy the heart of God to them. These areas are only concentration camps in disguise waiting for a vanguard of evangelists to invade. Behind their neon psychic signs, their red-light districts, and their loud, deafening music is a hidden army of recruits. Only when we begin to prophesy their destiny and purpose in Christ will they awake from their deadly slumber and be saved.

Joshua L. Chamberlain is perhaps most widely known for his role in holding the federal position on Little Round Top during the battle of Gettysburg. Chamberlain was an unassuming college professor from Maine. The Twentieth Maine was positioned at the far left of the line on Little Round Top. A number of Union officers were killed in the midst of the battle, including Colonel Vincent, Chamberlain's superior.

Chamberlain was now left in a desperate situation. Having been given an order by Vincent to hold the Union's ground at all cost and not to retreat, yet learning that his men's ammunition was virtually depleted, he had to make a quick decision. Chamberlain decided to counterattack and thus ordered a bayonet charge down the hill. The Union's position was saved. There was no time for conferencing and counsel; only swift confrontation would save the high ground.

Without confrontation there is no victory. There comes a time in every army when they must charge forward, when they must advance past enemy lines and take ground. It calls for great bravery and courage. Moses' orders to Joshua were straightforward: "Be strong and of a great courage; be not afraid, neither be overwhelmed, for the Lord your God is with you wherever you go" (Josh. 1:9). In this critical hour of human history, the church must now make her bayonet charge into the streets and cities of the world and push back the darkness that is threatening to prevail. We must take the high ground at all cost! We must invade the Samarias of the world, with our worship and our intercession transforming our conferences into all-out battle cries. Only then will we see the victories secured and the opening of the vast prisons to those who are bound.

Our greatest victories are yet ahead. God is putting his hand on normal people like Joshua Chamberlain to do exploits; could you be one? Are you willing to find your little piece of dirt and hold it? History is yet to be written by those who hear the great call of harvest and respond. Like arrows from the quiver of heaven, they will be aimed and shot into the nations and streets, flaming and igniting everything they touch.

Joshua Chamberlain said it best in his dedication of the Maine monument at Gettysburg on the evening of October 3, 1889: "In great deeds, something abides. On great fields, something stays. Forms change and pass; bodies disappear; but spirits linger, to consecrate ground for the vision-place of souls. And reverent men and women from afar, and generations that know us not and that we know not of, heart-drawn to see where and by whom great things were suffered and done for them, shall come to this deathless field, to ponder and dream; and lo! the shadow of a mighty presence shall wrap them in His bosom, and the power of the vision pass into their souls."

Chapter 19

Where Are the Evangelists?

*I believe that in each generation God has called
enough men and women to evangelize all the yet
unreached tribes of the earth.... It is not God who
does not call. It is man who will not respond!*
—Isobel Kuhn
Missionary to China and Thailand

When Paul penned those great words to Timothy, "do
the work of an evangelist," it was not a passing whim
or trivial thing; Paul had a motive. Prior to those convicting
words and the ageless call to evangelism, Paul evoked these
as well: "For the time will come when they will not endure
sound doctrine" (2 Tim. 4:3). You see, Paul knew that the
only preservation of the gospel of Jesus Christ in a world
full of imposters was through the pure channel of evangelism trailblazing across history through hearts aflame with
its message. It was the bedrock of their faith, and it was the
fire that burned across the dark recesses of time, refusing
to be snuffed out. Every other form of preaching fades and
often finds its own erroneous interpretations and doctrines.
In the darkest times of world events, it was the return to the

message of Jesus Christ, His death, burial, and resurrection, that catapulted a church back to grace.

It was during those times of what we call revival that the world emerged from intellectual and moral darkness as the church returned to her first love: the gospel of Jesus Christ. The condition of the world around us is hinged on this truth. When the church veers from its call to preach the gospel to all nations, its streets and cities, they will inevitably be swallowed up in spiritual and social depravity.

The only hope for the early church in Acts was not theology or prophecy; it was framed in their prayer as they faced the merciless onslaught of Roman and Jew alike: "And now, Lord, behold their threats: and grant unto thy servants, that with all boldness they may speak thy word, by stretching forth thine hand to heal; and that signs and wonders may be done by the name of thy holy child Jesus" (Acts 4:29–30). This was evangelism with power and validity that preserved the life and message of Jesus Christ despite the vise of unbelief and idolatry that attempted to destroy it.

There really is no room for argument. The providence of God knew that the only way to preserve His Word was through a people who lived it, preached it, and died for it. As Jesus stood at the threshold of leaving His own earthly ministry, He declared to the nucleus of what would become the church: "And he said unto them, Go ye into all the world, and preach the gospel to every creature" (Mark 16:15). It was the only way and is still the only way. Without this mandate, His message would have imploded and fizzled into a generational dispensational moment that would never have been able to leap the walls of Jewish culture, which tragically becomes the epitaph of many churches today.

The only hope then and now was a people who would go into all the world and preach the gospel. Where in our ascension have we lost this great commission? Where in our insatiable appetite for glory and gifts have we forfeited our inheritance? If God could ask a pertinent question even as you read this, could it be, *Where are the evangelists?*

Teaching has shipwrecked on the rocks of men's erroneous understanding, and prophecy has jettisoned past all reason to build its own kingdom; however, the pure fire of evangelism always finds its north. It is the compass of the kingdom of God, and it cannot be dimmed or deterred. It was and is the apostolic creed, in a world full of mystics and power brokers, that has anchored the church through every wind of doctrine. It is still the only truth to live and die by.

Can prophecy save you? Never. It may lead you, illuminate present truth to you, and give you a future and a hope. Yet current prophetic words or statements will never give access into the kingdom of God and eternal life. There is only one access point into that kingdom: the bloody, battered body of Christ and an empty tomb. Paul knew this, as he recorded in 1 Corinthian 13:8: "But whether there be prophecies, they shall fail." The unfailing love of God through Jesus Christ is still the hope of the world.

It would behoove us to remember the epic discourse of Paul: "Moreover, brethren, I declare unto you the gospel which I preached unto you, which also ye have received, and wherein ye stand; by which also ye are saved, if ye keep in memory what I preached unto you, unless ye have believed in vain. For I delivered unto you first of all that which I also received, how that Christ died for our sins according to the scriptures; and that he was buried, and that he rose again the third day according to the scriptures" (1 Cor. 15:1–4).

Have we believed in vain? Have we allowed current doctrines and self-perceived prophecies to cause us to abandon not only our first love but His? Have we so soon forgotten His message and what He died for and pursued "greater things"? When the church loses its direction, the passion to preach the gospel of Jesus Christ and redeem souls always gets it back on course. It is the binding force, the ligaments and sinews, that holds the body of Christ together.

Endlessly we will argue the validity of prophecy and its place in Scripture, and the rapture will continue to rattle the cages of modern theology; but the ancient yet timeless words of Christ burn across the sky of history to this day: "Jesus answered and said unto him, Verily, verily, I say unto thee, except a man be born again, he cannot see the kingdom of God" (John 3:3). Etch these words of Jesus on your heart as you pursue every high thing in this present world: "Marvel not that I said unto thee, Ye must be born again" (John 3:7).

Chapter 20

The Philip Factor

God is a God of missions. He wills missions. He commands missions. He demands missions. He made missions possible through His Son. He made missions actual in sending the Holy Spirit.
— George W. Peters

Philip was just like you. He didn't have any elaborate organization or planning, not even a polished itinerary with accommodations and an adoring audience waiting for him. According to history, he had very little at his disposal, with the exception of faith and the power of the Holy Spirit. Today we are often expected to have website and high-profile endorsements with every convenience at our finger-tips before we are even considered to do what Philip did. Philip had one simple strategy—he went.

What awaited him at the end of his journey is the outcome every Christian should hope and live for: revival. In one sweeping moment, all that Philip was and is was consum-mated into one sentence: "And the people with one accord gave heed to the things which Philip spoke, hearing and seeing the miracles which he did" (Acts 8:6).

Can you imagine an entire city listening and following the gospel message that you preach, with entire city blocks and neighborhoods confessing Jesus Christ? Once you can accept the possibility of this in your own day-to-day life and that Philip was really no different from any of us today, then you are well on your way to exponentially experiencing revival in all its wonder and power at any moment.

Let's rewind just a little bit and find out exactly what Philip *did* have so that we can comprehend how he had such a concentrated impact in such a short period of time. In Acts 6:5, Philip appears on center stage. Two words mark him and give us a glimpse into his spiritual DNA that later propelled him into revival history: "a man full of *faith* and the *Holy Ghost.*" (Acts 6:5).

Faith is the catalyst to any move of God, and the power of the Holy Spirit unleashed into human form has the ability to take normal circumstances and amplify them to historical proportions. That is exactly what happened when Jesus met the woman at Jacob's well in what appeared at first glance to be a normal, predictable situation. As the Holy Spirit framed that moment, it was transformed from a mundane encounter to a full-blown regional revival. Philip was no different, and neither are you.

What challenged the church centuries ago still challenges it today. When Philip went down to the city of Samaria and preached Christ to them there was an unimaginable gap between the church of Acts and the Samaritan-Gentile non-Jewish world. That gap has only widened over the centuries as man continues to distance itself in every manner of the word from the very world or "Samaria" it is called to reach. What caused Philip to suddenly rise up from the current circumstances of death and persecution and literally re-write current doctrine? It was clearly understood the gospel of that day was a Jewish one, Jesus had proved that. Now in a blink of an eye and one underage religious rebel of his time gets up and leaps the invisible gap between him and revival and changes history.

The threshold of every revival is found in Acts 8:5: "Then Philip went." The greatest stumbling block for any pursuer of harvest is the inability to go. We are faced with an obstacle course of excuses and resisters who argue from every angle why we shouldn't, are not able to, and cannot. But the thin red line of revival is always there, waiting for one person to cross over into its wonder and power. Religion and routine divorced themselves long ago from spontaneity and have sunken the vehicle of revival in red tape and formality, leaving a generation of revivalists waiting impatiently in the prayer lines. Philip finally just *went,* and in that act of going, an entire city was lit up with the insatiable flames of revival.

Uninvited, no afterglow of ordination – Philip just got up and went. Suddenly the DNA of history was radically changed. From Jewish Law, one obedient act of a young man named Philip catapulted the church into the future and bridged the gap between Jerusalem and Samaria shattering prejudice and dogma. The ancient rift between the "Church" and ultimately the world to which it was sent to save was crossed. The margin between church and street was narrowed dramatically as one young evangelist leapt the ancient religious hurdles that lay before him.

Now picture yourself in the most ordinary situation this very day, somewhere between one appointment and the next, with twenty minutes to spare in any random public venue. Hurry, look around you! Revival is peering through veiled eyes and darkened hearts, waiting for the flint and stone of divine appointment. In these undefined moments that are glossed over and hurried past, revival sits idle, like dry kindling waiting for the spark. If you are the light and they are in the dark, this creates a criterion that is absolutely perfect for the power of God to be displayed. It is simply hinged on your awareness of them and the willingness to speak.

Pray right now that the same fire that burned off the restraints of tradition from Philip would do the same for you. Today could be your entrance into a history making moment as the world around you becomes a field of promise not routine. You are God's catalyst of opportunity and you can either pray, *"Here am I send me"* or you can drown in an ocean of importunity. The driving force of God's power can propel you as it did Philip into unbelievable moments of divine appointment leaving an indelible mark on mankind. You are God's instrument of harvest and revival and you can make a dramatic difference today as you simply accept His call to go. Hurry look around you! Joy is waiting to invade and transform the predictable landscape of your life and bring the Kingdom of God to earth.

Chapter 21

Do You Have a Shadow?

*I have but one candle of life to burn, and I would
rather burn it out in a land filled with darkness than
in a land flooded with light.*
　　　　　　　　　　　　　　　—John Keith Falconer

In a world of mass convenience and jet-set ideas, it's hard
to imagine that revival needs no more than an obedient
heart and a body that it beats in. Peter did not need a venue
or a prayer line; people on beds and couches simply filled the
streets, waiting for him to pass by. The question is, Do you
have a heart filled with Jesus? Do you have hands willing
to touch and reach out to pray with someone? Do you have
a mouth wide open that He can fill with words of truth and
grace? Then revival is at your fingertips. If you have a body
to cast a shadow and the love of Jesus burning in your spirit
inside that body, then you are at the razor's edge of transformation. Everything else is just convenient.

My first year as a Christian, I had two things at my
disposal: an old, faded white leather Bible and the insatiable
fire within me to preach the gospel of Jesus. Armed with these
two weapons, I saw a criminal institution of 150 inmates,
where I was also a resident, saved. I would kneel hour after

hour at the foot of my steel bed in a small eight-by-twelve-foot cell and pray. Once the doors opened, I would walk the institution, imploring all that would hear that salvation was as simple as asking.

In that one year, when I was the fragile age of seventeen, with absolutely no formal training or instruction except for the vivid testimonies found in the Bible, God proved to me that revival was not only possible but simple to anyone who would step out to meet it. After twenty years and countless revival experiences, this implacable fact still remains the same: God just needs a body and heart to fill with His Spirit and power, and a world to send it to. Is revival calling out to you?

Let's look at Acts 5:15: "Insomuch that they brought the sick into the streets, and laid them on beds and couches that at least the shadow of Peter passing by might overshadow some of them." The principal outcome of revival was not overshadowed by altars and steeples, but to the contrary, it was in the dank open air of Jerusalem's streets, in the shadow of a new breed of healers and priests. They were not confined to ritual or regimen that blotted out their shadow and neatly put them under a bushel.

Streets and squares were the stages where Christ was put on display, and the city laid its broken and battered in their way. You, too, have a shadow, and your streets can become the arena where it's cast as the light of His love shines down. Grab your Bible and your backpack and exit your prayer closet—it is curtain call, and you are on center stage as a great cloud of witnesses cheers you on. The words of Jesus are our rallying cry as we stand in the shadow of the Almighty: "Go into all the world and preach the gospel to every creature.... and lo I am with you always" (Mark 16:15; Matt. 28:20).

Chapter 22

Your Pulpit Is the Garbage Cans; Your Parish, the Alleys

"I have but one candle of life to burn, and I would rather burn it out in a land filled with darkness than in a land flooded with light."
—John Keith Falconer

The title of this chapter, "Your pulpit is the garbage cans; your parish, the alleys," were the words the Lord spoke to my heart in 1988 as I stood on the concrete garbage cans in downtown Seattle and ministered. Often large crowds would gather; other times they raced past, following some invisible gravity pulling them to their next point of interest. Police buses would often park on Second and Pike street waiting for the riots and arrests that would shortly follow in the crime ridden downtown district of Seattle. From this backdrop, we cut our teeth.

In those days, you could smell and taste revival. It was salty, blowing off the ocean and filling the air, accompanied by a myriad of sounds. Revival was not an objective—it was a life that we lived every night when the sun set and the people began to gather in the seedy city streets. We lived for it like a beggar craves a dollar; we left our place of prayer each night and stepped into the rarefied air of revival.

Just like a photographer needs a backdrop to capture a picture, revivalists need the open air of the world around them. They cannot be contained in the stale air of a building where everything is rationed and measured; they realize that revival is as spontaneous as the universe around them and filled with endless possibilities and action. If you are hungry for God to move and to see firsthand His power on display resulting in human contact and change, then you must break free from the orbit of church and its galaxy of time-consuming programs. Find a nursing home, a jailhouse, a coffee shop, a street corner, a Boys and Girls Club—anywhere that people are and the need for salvation is prevalent. You don't need to stand in the winding line of ordination waiting for a chance at the pulpit; remember, "The earth is the Lord's, and the fulness thereof" (Ps. 24:1). The world is your backdrop, and all of humanity is the audience—go discover this new world today.

Let me show in a couple of paragraphs how real this can be. I was in Pioneer Square, and I met a team member of a locally based outreach group whom I had seen before. Another young man accompanied her and stepped forward with his Bible in his hand and introduced himself: "Do you remember me?" I did not. He was nicely dressed and appeared to be well informed about the streets and carried himself like a seasoned evangelist. He leaned forward again and said, "You don't remember me?"

It hit me. Two weeks ago, after most of the city had shut down, we were still looking for souls—anyone who would pray with us and hear about Jesus. We finally resorted to the Greyhound bus terminal downtown, and there we found the gold: two runaway teenagers, cold, hungry, and alone. After a powerful time of prayer, as both received Jesus, we gave them what we could and left. Two weeks later, a bedraggled, homeless teen was now carrying a Bible and was enrolled in a local church's ministry training class. This was the young man standing in front of me, Bible in hand and on fire. God could do in two short weeks what the machine of religion cannot; that is, ignite the inherent gift of Jesus in every saved person, thus putting him or her on a straight course for revival. This was in the fall of 1989. Imagine what is possible now...

Remember, the world is your parish, and every human heart is the page of your testimony ready to be written. What are you waiting for?

Chapter 23

Is Fear a Factor for You?

God isn't looking for people of great faith, but for individuals ready to follow Him.
— Hudson Taylor

There is nothing more numbing and incapacitating to the work of the Holy Spirit in an individual than fear. Fear freezes and chains a spirit to the whipping post of inadequacy, making the person feel inferior and grossly insufficient. One of the most frequently heard comments as I travel and help people step out into the real world and express their passion for Jesus is this: "I am afraid of rejection," or "I am not sure what to do or say." The smoke and mirror of fear have them incapacitated and completely unable to move forward in their faith. As fear continues to run its course in these Christians' lives, inevitably they have to then create or find doctrines or beliefs to support their constant resistance to take up their cross and follow Jesus.

The entire fabric of the gospel of Jesus from Matthew through John, and carried through with incredible clarity in the Acts of the apostles, is the inescapable mandate to go, to preach, to teach all nations, and to bring an unbelieving world to the knowledge of Jesus Christ. It's undeniable, and you simply cannot get around it—unless… you begin to build an elaborate checks-and-balances system of rationale that excuses you from the table of obedience that clearly commands, "Go into all the world and preach the gospel."

Paul elaborated on this responsibility in Romans 10:14–15: "How can they call on Him whom they have never believed, and how can they believe on Him whom they have never heard? And how shall they hear without a preacher? *And how shall they preach unless they are sent?*" (emphasis added). As maintained by Scripture, the only way the world will ever know that Jesus Christ is Lord is for you to go, and you have to open your mouth and speak.

As fear continues its winding course through your heart, it builds a house of cards that resists the inner call to go and preach. It sets up schemes such as, "I am not called," "It's not my calling," and "I am called to the church." The fallacy is that the church is only represented in buildings that are titled churches or have some other religious verbiage; Jesus called His followers, the ones on whom He would build the church so that the gates of hell could not prevail against it, from the docks, seashores, and city streets.

The church He defined was not only in the synagogue and its hallowed corridors; it was among the thieves, prostitutes, and tax collectors. How does that translate into modern day? It is the biker, druggie, businessman, gothic, punk, skater, housewife, surfer, bum, and the entire kaleidoscope of humanity that rushes by us every day.

Current movements, such as the prophetic in which I am intimately involved every day, often run the greatest risk of losing their bearings from the world around them. We can become so revelatory and deep, ever seeking the next vision or revelation, that we completely and often purposefully forget the call of God to preach. The prophetic people of our time must first realize that every gift stated in the New Testament is ultimately intended to call a world to Jesus, transforming them into the body of Christ and growing them up into Jesus Christ.

It's no surprise that the apostolic ministry of Paul declared, "So I have strived to preach the gospel, not where Christ was named, unless I should build upon another man's foundation." (Romans 15:20). Paul realized the dynamic that the church had to be built, and in order to build anything, you have to go out and find the raw material to build it with. Don't let fear be a factor for you as the finish line of harvest calls out to you to join the race of eternity. Clear the table of excuses and go!

Chapter 24

The Coming Persecution

We talk of the second coming; half the world has never heard of the first.
—Oswald J. Smith

We are entering a greater level of His power that will be accompanied by a greater level of persecution. I was reviewing some of the persecution of our heroes of the Bible, such as Paul, David, Moses, and others. Do you realize much of their persecution was reasonable and even justifiable? David murdered and committed adultery, actions that would warrant imprisonment and making the tabloids today. In other words, there was every reason to persecute him; yet David was still a man after God's own heart and chosen of God as a king.

Moses murdered, abandoned his family in Egypt, and fell from his lofty position of ministry and authority. Paul was a mass murderer, as he carried death warrants for Christians' arrest, lampooning the early church. There was every moral and legal reason to hound these early Christians, but God chose the foolish things to confound the wise, nonetheless. Their present persecution put them in a place of greater grace and glory. We do not often associate that with God's blessing today, do we? It's easier to gravitate toward the long prayer lines for blessing and prosperity than embrace persecution and rejection.

"And they departed from the presence of the council, rejoicing that they were counted worthy to suffer shame for his name" (Acts 5:41). They were persecuted for the preaching of the Word; however, they were also breaking the law of the land by preaching it! It's the lifestyle that these people lived that merited the persecution that deemed them fit for the honor of suffering shame for His name. Anyone who desires a greater glory must realize it will cost everything, including reputation and status, or it isn't His glory after all. "Forasmuch then as Christ hath suffered for us in the flesh, arm yourselves likewise with the same mind: for he that hath suffered in the flesh hath ceased from sin" (1 Pet. 4:1).

Today in contemporary mind-sets, it's who esteems you that qualifies you for ministry or Christian service. We pass out Christian résumés and accolades; in Paul's day, it was quite different: "Being defamed, we intreat: we are made as the filth of the world, and are the offscouring of all things unto this day. I write not these things to shame you, but as my beloved sons I warn you" (1 Cor. 4:13–14).

This same warning is echoing through history today. It is looking at us in our well-to-do faces and beseeching, "Are you ready to die? Are you ready to lose everything for the call? Are you prepared to be hated and scorned so as to be entrusted with My secret treasures of grace and power?" We must pass through the eye of the needle of suffering and persecution if we desire to enter into the fields of favor and harvest that are waiting for this generation.

In the New Testament landscape, it was the ones who hated and despised you that set you apart for ministry rather than the ones who loved and adored you. In light of Luke 6, I wonder who really is qualified for service: "Woe unto you, when all men shall speak well of you! For so did their fathers to the false prophets" (Luke 6:26).

Paul faced the same dilemma in his time, as many were clamoring for Christian service and position. Men desired position more than they desired His power. Shouldn't it be the moral and spiritual climate over our cities that is changing rather than our worrying about who dislikes or likes us? "But if I do, though ye believe not me, believe the works: that you may know, and believe, that the Father is in me, and I in him" (John 10:38).

Everything that appears to be good today could be hated tomorrow. We must strip ourselves of this modern-day theology of approval and disapproval and begin to see people through Christ's eyes. Jesus defined this kind of generation: "To what, then, can I compare the people of this generation? What are they like? They are like children sitting in the marketplace and calling out to each other: 'We played the flute for you, and you did not dance; we sang a dirge, and you did not cry.' For John the Baptist came neither eating bread nor drinking wine, and you say, 'He has a demon.' The Son of Man came eating and drinking, and you say, 'Here is a glutton and a drunkard, a friend of tax collectors and sinners' " (Luke 7:31–34).

Things are never what they appear to be. The scales of modern-day thinking must be peeled off and the eyes of our understanding enlightened if we are ever to see clearly the radical generation that is now appearing. Even the ancient prophet Samuel had to have this predetermined mind-set taken away. He was looking at appearances to determine who was approved or disapproved by God, and he nearly missed the king! "But the LORD said to Samuel, 'Do not consider his appearance or his height, for I have rejected him. The LORD does not look at the things man looks at. Man looks at the outward appearance, but the LORD looks at the heart' "(1 Sam. 16:7).

The characters who will lead the march into harvest at this junction will be the ones often rejected by man and the status quo. They will be the misfits and the offscouring. They will not have chosen this road—no one ever does—but it will be the cross that faces them on their journey of destiny. Many will turn away from this cross of persecution and rejection and will go back to more comfortable climates, but others will count the cost and write the future's history books. Like John the Baptist, they will pledge their heads to heaven. It is time to gird ourselves and arm ourselves with the mind of Christ; only then will we see beyond these portals of persecution into the fields of His favor. God, grant Your servants this grace.

"For many walk, of whom I have told you often, and now tell you even weeping, that they are the enemies of the cross of Christ: whose end is destruction, whose god is their belly, and whose glory is in their shame—who set their mind on earthly things" (Phil. 3:18–19).

Chapter 25

The Woman at the River of Consequence

The reason some folks don't believe in missions is that the brand of religion they have isn't worth propagating.

—Author unknown

As I was meditating today regarding the United States and the various places I have visited and what is happening currently, I saw the following vision: A woman, with large clay pots and wineskin-type bags to fill with water, was going to a river. She looked tired but still determined to get the water from the river back to the house up the hill behind her. She faithfully and carefully filled each container and proceeded to carry them up, one by one, to her house. To her dismay, though, when she arrived back at her house up the steep hill, the pots and containers were nearly empty. There were no apparent holes in these containers, yet they were still empty. She kept going back down to the river over and over and over again to fill her pots with water. Each time she would arrive back home with little more than enough water for her and her family to have a few sips, and then it was gone. This left her household discouraged, frustrated, and never satisfied, so she kept going back to the river to repeat the same process over and over again.

This is what the Lord told me as I saw this vision of the woman with the pots: "The woman with the pots is the church. The river is My presence and My Spirit. The pots and wineskins are the methods and ways the church goes to receive from Me. The household is the body of Christ, the lost, and the cities the church is trying to serve. She never has enough supply to really satisfy the deep hunger of her city or her own people, so she keeps going back to the river to refill her containers. The only way the church will ever be able to fill herself up and keep herself filled is to *give away what she already has.* She cannot continue to hoard and try to store up My anointing any longer. I will not allow it. The harvest is too white, and the time is too short. *She must give it away to keep it!"*

The Lord reminded me of the widow in Elijah's day when there was a great drought in the land (see 2 Kings 17). She was so determined to bake her last meal for herself and her household and then die. Her only means to survive the drought, according to Elijah, was *to give away what little she already had!* This is the same challenge the Lord is giving to the church of America in this hour. We cannot afford to hoard our anointing, or "water," any longer.

Our conferences, churches, and modern-day meetings have literally become this parable: "And he spake a parable unto them, saying, The ground of a certain rich man brought forth plentifully: and he thought within himself, saying, What shall I do, because I have no room where to bestow my fruits? And he said, This will I do: I will pull down my barns, and build greater; and there will I bestow all my fruits and my goods. And I will say to my soul, Soul, thou hast much goods laid up for many years; take thine ease, eat, drink, and be merry" (Luke 12:16–19). As the prophet Amos said so long ago, we are "at ease in Zion." (Amos 6:1)

We continue to stage bigger and better conferences and meetings, build bigger and brighter ministries and churches, and yet the very cities we are doing this in are still lost, thirsty, and desperate. As ministers and ministries, we *must* see this and admit our fault. We have been in a state of denial and pride, unwilling to admit our failure and move on. Our cities and streets, overall, are untouched and void of any real, genuine impact.

Walk downtown sometime in your city at midnight and see for yourself. Visit a local bar this weekend and take notes. Go to the local mall and stand near the youth who hang out there and see. The cities are *not* impacted by our current methods and approaches to conferences and meetings. Before we can really move on, we must have the courage as leaders to admit this.

This is the Lord's reply to our denial: "But God said unto him, Thou fool, this night thy soul shall be required of thee: then whose shall those things be, which thou hast provided? So is he that layeth up treasure for himself, and is not rich toward God"

(Luke 12:20–21). Our "souls," or our ministries, will be required of us. In other words, the Lord is going to ask us: "Did My harvest get taken in during your conferences and meetings? Did you visit the widows and orphans in their affliction? When I was naked, did you clothe Me? When I was hungry, did you feed Me? When I was in prison and sick, did you visit Me?" Every one of us will be asked those questions.

We need to begin posthaste to train and raise up teams in our conferences and meetings to reach the cities, streets, and neighborhoods that we are convening in. Our conferences have become private parties where the lost and misled generation feels uncomfortable and out of place. Everything we do in our meetings caters to the Christian and the saved. We have lost the purpose of Christ as seen in His meetings and gatherings in ancient Israel: "And when the Pharisees saw it, they said unto his disciples, Why eateth your Master with publicans and sinners? But when Jesus heard that, he said unto them, They that be whole need not a physician, but they that are sick. But go ye and learn what that meaneth, I will have mercy, and not sacrifice: for I am not come to call the righteous, but sinners to repentance" (Matt 9:11–13).

We have used the excuse of "we are equipping the church" for too long. Equipping them to do what? Sing better? Pray better? Prophesy better? We must train and mobilize the church for harvest, equip them and enable them to save a soul, to talk to a stranger, to lead someone to Jesus. That is the greatest form of ministry there is. We must introduce the church to evangelism, thus releasing them into an anointing where they can prophesy the destiny of people, places, and cities. Until we have done that, we are falling short of the Great Commission of Jesus that still echoes through time today: "And he said unto them, Go ye into all the world, and preach the gospel to every creature" (Mark 16:15). That is the most prophetic and apostolic statement ever declared.

The woman in the vision at the beginning of this chapter represents all of us, trying so hard to keep something that was never meant for us to keep. Jesus made it very clear: freely receive, freely give. This must be the precedent we set this year in our conferences and meetings. If we can go home with a clear conscience night after night, week after week, never *giving away that precious supply,* then we will be the recipients of Jesus' words to the church of Laodicea: "I know thy works, that thou art neither cold nor hot: I would thou wert cold or hot. So then because thou art lukewarm, and neither cold nor hot, I will spue thee out of my mouth" (Rev. 3:15–16).

In the vision, the river is the Lord, and we need to be filled by it every day. But if, as leaders, pastors, prophets, and ministers, we are not first getting our feet wet and leading the people into the harvest, then we are doing an injustice to eternity; and our ministries and anointing will be required of us.

Listen to the ancient instructions of Joshua to his era of elders and leaders: "And it shall come to pass, as soon as the soles of the feet of the priests that bear the ark of the LORD, the LORD of all the earth, shall rest in the waters of Jordan, that the waters of Jordan shall be cut off from the waters that come down from above; and they shall stand upon an heap" (Josh. 3:13). Joshua 3:13 is a prophetic mandate for leadership in this nation. *We must step out first and get our own feet wet and lead the people over the Jordan to possess the land!* We cannot afford to hide behind generic excuses any longer; we must do it.

Are we ready to confront the consequence of our disobedience: the blood of millions on the hands of our present-day ministries? We must act now. I quote the words of William Booth, founder and prophet of the Salvation Army, and pray the fire of the Holy Spirit burns the fetters of indifference away:

There have been more than enough conferences, and congresses, and committees, and deliberations. It is time to act! There is not a moment to lose! There cannot be any question to what we have to do. No more conferences! No more doubt! No more delay! Arise, ye children of the light, and buckle on the armor bright, and now prepare yourselves to fight, against the world and Satan. We are called to be saints. We are called to be brothers and sisters of Jesus, to fight with Him, for Him, with every particle of strength we have to the last grasp. That is enough! No more conferences! (January 1876)

Chapter 26

A Kairos Moment

If you found a cure for cancer, wouldn't it be inconceivable to hide it from the rest of mankind? How much more inconceivable to keep silent the cure from the eternal wages of death.

—Dave Davidson

*K*airos is an ancient Greek word meaning the "right or opportune moment" or "God's time." The ancient Greeks had two words for time, *chronos* and *kairos*. While *chronos* refers to chronological or sequential time, *kairos* signifies "a time in between," or a moment of an undetermined period of time in which something significant or special happens. One definition defines it as *"a passing instant when an opening appears which must be driven through with force if success is to be achieved."* A *kairos* moment is not just a sovereign moment outside our control or achievement, but the contrary is at work here. It's a moment in time and history that must be seized and taken advantage of and pressed through with immediate action.

In Old Testament times, there were descendants of Jacob who epitomized this: "And of the children of Issachar, which were men that had understanding of the times, to know what

Israel ought to do" (1 Chron. 12:32). Jesus, also, identified a *kairos* moment when He wept over Jerusalem; unfortunately, they failed to see or discern this: "Now as He drew near, He saw the city and wept over it, saying, 'If you had known, even you, especially in this your day, the things that make for your peace! But now they are hidden from your eyes... *because you did not know the time of your visitation*" (Luke 19:41–44, emphasis added). They failed to see and seize their *kairos* moment.

How many times has a *kairos* moment been hidden from your eyes? The greater question would be, What causes our *kairos* moments to be hidden? Paul experienced a *kairos* moment, yet scales remained on his eyes until Ananias prayed for him. This could be seen as a *kairos* moment for the entire church, as the Lord suddenly converted its greatest opponent and made him its greatest proponent. Ananias knew this and went after it in prayer and obedience. *Kairos* moments are revealed through prayer and then completed in obedience. One cannot fulfill the *kairos* moment absent of the other. Often we can get ensnared in the thinking that prayer alone can steer a *kairos* moment into fulfillment, or that action and activity can do the same.

We see both of these dynamics in action in another *kairos* moment: "But that you may know that the Son of Man has power on Earth to forgive sins—then He said to the paralytic, 'Arise, take up your bed, and go to your house.' And he arose and departed to his house. Now when the multitudes saw it, they marveled and glorified God, who had given such power to men" (Matt. 9:6–8).

Prayer and the declaration of faith put that paralytic man's *kairos* moment into action, but it was not completed until "he arose and departed to his house." You see, *kairos* moments need prayer with action infused with it. In Acts 2, they were all "in one accord and in prayer," but they also *"went everywhere preaching the word"* (Acts 8:4, emphasis added). This present *kairos* moment that hangs in the balance for the entire world hinges on prayer and your own personal action. You must move forward and put visible, viable action to your inspiration, and the result will be no less than those in biblical times.

Kairos also means, in *Strong's Concordance,* "a set or proper time: a fixed or special occasion, opportunity, or due season; *an individual opportunity, season, or space"* (emphasis added). "On the day the LORD gave the Israelites victory over the Amorites, Joshua prayed to the LORD in front of all the people of Israel. He said, 'Let the sun stand still over Gibeon, and the moon over the valley of Aijalon.' So the sun and moon stood still until the Israelites had defeated their enemies" (Josh. 10:12–13). In a *kairos* moment, time is no factor on the divine results. In this "individual opportunity, season, or space" for Joshua, the entire universe stood with bated breath as the battle was won.

When you step into a *kairos* moment, everything works in your favor, clearing the road before you. The problem is that most do not discern their season or opportunity and, like Jerusalem, miss their own day of visitation. Entire cities and regions sit in spiritual decay, never realizing that the day of their visitation and *kairos* moment is right now. We must quantum leap with prayer and personal action until the will of God is fulfilled.

Look at another *kairos* moment in Matthew 27. In a *kairos* moment, heaven and Earth can collide at a crossroads where two worlds converge. The lines that divide the temporal and the invisible blur, and to differentiate between the two can be impossible. Look at verses 50–53 for a moment to see a panoramic *kairos* moment: "Then Jesus shouted out again, and he gave up his spirit. At that moment the curtain in the temple was torn in two, from top to bottom. The earth shook, rocks split apart, and tombs opened. The bodies of many godly men and women who had died were raised from the dead after Jesus' resurrection. They left the cemetery, went into the holy city of Jerusalem and appeared to many people."

Remember, it is a moment or *"a passing instant when an opening appears which must be driven through with force if success is to be achieved."* When the most climatic *kairos* moment in history hit the world like a runaway train, the veil was torn in two, the earth quaked, graves were literally opened, and the dead rose to life again. As we approach many more *kairos* moments in our own personal lives and as a corporate church, we, too, must drive through with force, or rather seize the moment and move forward.

When Jesus stated to His disciples, "The harvest *is* great," He was revealing a *kairos* moment from then until now. It is a harvest produced by prophecy that we are to fulfill. This prophetic harvest that Jesus declared in Luke 4 is profound: "Do not say, There are yet four months, and then cometh harvest. Behold, I say unto you, Lift up your eyes, and look on the fields; for they are white already to harvest. And he that reaped receives wages, and gathers fruit unto life eternal: that both he that sowed and he that reaped may rejoice together" (John 4:35–36).

The *kairos* moment for the harvest that Jesus declared is *now*. It's not later—it's right now. That *kairos* moment is still waiting for a generation of present-day Christians to fully seize its potential and realize we are a "time in between" from His departure and return; and ultimately, the reaping of this prophetic harvest will determine its completion. "And this gospel of the kingdom shall be preached in all the world for a witness unto all nations; and then shall the end come" (Matt. 24:14).

Can you imagine an entire church generation coming into one accord in a *kairos* moment and leaping the walls of predetermined doctrine to preach this gospel to all nations? We would undoubtedly be "looking for and hasting unto the coming of the day of God" (2 Pet. 3:12). Can you come to the awesome conclusion right now that you are a harvester and harbinger of His harvest of souls upon the earth? Will you relinquish your rights and ambitions and say with Isaiah, "Here I am; send me!"

Right now, you can qualify as one of those laborers that Jesus stated were few compared to the harvest that faced them. You can expedite the coming of Jesus Christ to this present Earth by simply praying right now: "Lord, make me Your harvester. Make me Your servant; make me Your living sacrifice." Harvest is waiting for you right outside your door; your only limitation is the amount you desire to reap. As those great missionaries before you, give vivaciously, give completely, and the eternal rewards will far outweigh the menial forfeitures you make right now. *Go!* What do you have to lose? Now look what you have to gain!

Chapter 27

Revival, Small-Town America

For who has despised the day of small things? For they shall rejoice.
—Zechariah 4:10

This message is twofold. First, it is a brief report of what we have been seeing across the nation in small-town America, small cities and towns, many with populations of only 250. Second, it is a prophetic glimpse into the future of national revival and reformation. One such place was in Paisley, Oregon, where we experienced this phenomenon of revival in a seemingly obscure and small city.

In this tiny town with a population of only 250, God reached the world. Let me explain. In this city was an international dormitory of high school exchange students from around the globe, from places like Bosnia, Korea, China, Russia, Mongolia, Sweden, Switzerland, and Japan, just to name a few. Only two students were saved when we arrived; all were saved when we left. God reached the world in four days.

The paradox is this: God is moving wherever there is a hunger for Him and desperation for salvation—not only in the metropolitan cites, but in the rural areas as well.

God is reaching into wherever there is a beacon of prayer beaming into heaven and an insatiable appetite to see people rescued.

Bethlehem was a case study on greatness, as the Spirit of God chose the most obscure and underqualified to host His Son. The same dynamic applies to the tiny towns, villages, and rural spaces that fill the volume of any map. From these "mangers," God is preparing missionaries, evangelists, and trailblazers who will see the far-flung borders of the world as their target.

Shortly after we were in Paisley, we were in Battle Mountain, Nevada, another small, seemingly forgotten place. Again the phenomena of revival began to break out as hunger superseded tradition. From unconventional Methodist churches to Pentecostal parishes, it is the same: a great hunger for revival and harvest. The cry of harvest is reaching a crescendo: *"God, we need revival. We cannot traverse from Sunday to Sunday any longer! We need a move of God!"*

In Kettle Falls, Washington, with no more than twenty in our meetings, God moved dramatically. From the church to the local bar, God was appearing. Again, this was a town hardly on the map; yet the desire of the people superseded numbers and crowds. Souls were being saved, and people began to gather from all around.

We are getting emails every day from obscure and out-of-the-way places to come and partner in harvest and revival. My answer is the same to every one: "Yes!" Jesus revealed His heart when He made the statement "leave the ninety-nine for the one" (Matt. 18:12). In this hour, the greatest glory will be found with the one, the individual making his or her mark in the great harvest field as a colaborer with Jesus Himself. Most will still pursue the ninety-nine, but the secret treasure of revival will be found with the one, the few, and the infrequent.

Many well-known leaders will begin to hear the call from Bethlehem. They will see the divine destiny in these small cities and places and go without price or figure. They will be like the man who found the hidden treasure in the field and gave all he had to secure it.

Many treasures of revival are hidden in small-town America. A few of the mainline ministries are about to discover the wealth of these hidden places. The allure of large offerings will not compel them, but rather the eternal weight of glory hidden in these towns will draw them. These small places will become headquarters and staging grounds for international revival and missions training. They will have an incredible revelation of missions and outreach. They will send thousands into the uttermost parts of the earth.

These small towns will also produce some of the future's most prolific leaders and missionaries. A passion of harvest will resound in the hearts of these young people. The temptation of the age will not seduce them. They will rise from the shadow of obscurity to shine like the star that led the men to the manger. They will exponentially excel in academics where other larger cities are struggling, proving God's favor is upon them. This will garner the attention of media and government and only help to fuel the fires of revival.

Generations of prayer and prophecies in these small towns will now begin to be rapidly fulfilled. Not one jot or tittle will fall to the ground empty, but rather a great harvest of promise is about to occur in *small-town America*. Even now, great Christian political leaders are being prepared for public service in these areas. They will adhere to the morals of their forefathers and the convictions of Christ. They will bring revival to the political arena.

Small-town America will be on the map of history's greatest revivals. In the Bible Belt in particular, a great grace for unity will be poured out as the walls of adherent tradition give way. Walls that have separated Baptist and Pentecostal will fall flat. Charismatic and conservative will stand together to see this great catch of harvest come in. The racial scars will be healed and washed as the unseemly lines of racism disappear. A great chain of unity will connect black and white, Baptist and Pentecostal, Lutheran and Methodist. It will set a spiritual precedent for the whole nation. It will set in motion racial reconciliation and revival. "Arise and shine, for your light has come, and the glory of the Lord is risen upon you" (Isa. 60:1). God is coming down to small-town America.

Chapter 28

The Lord of the Harvest

Tell the students to give up their small ambitions and come eastward to preach the gospel of Christ.
— Francis Xavier
Missionary to India, the Philippines, and Japan

When Jesus went up the mountain with three of His disciples, He was transfigured, or altered, from His human state to a glorified one. It was a fearful moment of splendor as the Son of Man revealed His heavenly identity and manifested His glory in human form to three trembling witnesses. The description of Jesus' appearance in this indescribable moment is life-changing and reveals a glimpse into the disciples' future shortly after this transfiguration.

Moments after this earth-shaking experience, as God the Father was heard audibly from heaven and Elijah and Moses appeared on the mountain with the Lord, Jesus declared to His disciples, "Tell the vision to no man *until* the Son of Man is risen from the dead." (Matt. 17:9) This indicated that there would be a time that this manifest presence of Jesus in all its blinding brilliance would be revealed and exposed to the world existing just below this mountaintop experience.

Now look a little closer at this event as the Gospel records it: "His face shone like the sun, and His raiment was white as the light." The word *shone* is a derivative from the Greek word *lampos,* which means "to shine with brilliance." The color of His clothing was as white as the light, which is *leukos,* the word for "white light" or fire." Jesus had become a brilliant, radiant white flame that caused the disciples to collapse to the ground in terror. This was not just a momentary passing experience, but rather a prophetic keyhole into the future that would be accessible to all after His resurrection. But as you will see, there was another hinge on this door of His glorious transfiguring presence: *the harvest.*

This was not the last time that this brilliant glory would be revealed. Fast forward a few chapters to Matthew 28. We see a vacant grave where the body of Jesus had been laid, and now, rather than Moses and Elijah appearing, the angel of the Lord descends, rolls the stone away from the cavity, and sits down. The angel announces to the two women who had come to fulfill their duties that Christ is not dead, but very much alive, and then commands them to "go quickly and tell His disciples that He risen from the dead!" (Matt. 28:7)

This is the first evangelistic mandate after Jesus conquered the grave, as the news of His resurrection raced through Galilee. When the angel commanded them to go, literally "two by two," we again see the same *white/leukos,* or brilliant light that is white like snow and bright as lightning. The angel appeared in the same glory that Jesus revealed on the Mount of Transfiguration and sent the two women to go with a message. What was once contained on the top of the mountain to three trembling disciples was now unveiled to the world. Mary Magdalene and her accomplice became the first evangelists proclaiming the resurrected Christ in the *leukos,* or His manifest power that His disciples had seen on the mountaintop.

Suddenly the vision begins to come into focus; the awesome presence and power revealed to the world in all of His amazing glory on the mountain then later at the empty grave are for a much larger, dynamic purpose. These manifestations were not just showcasing His stunning brilliance, but rather they were to confirm His resurrection and life to the world, past, present, and future. The glory of God revealed in these epic encounters was the sole spearhead of evangelism that would be confirmed with great signs and wonders.

This becomes even more clear as we hear the description of the harvest as Jesus exhorts His apostles, "Do not say there are yet four months and then comes the harvest. I say to you lift up your eyes, and look on the fields; *for they are* **white** *already for harvest"* (John 4:35, emphasis and bolding added). Did you see it? The same Greek word used at the Mount of Transfiguration to describe His glory and the same vivid language at the empty grave of a resurrected Jesus now define the harvest—*leukos: brilliant white light and fire!* A progressive advancement of God's presence was manifesting in the earth from the mountain, to the grave, and now in the harvest.

"And with great power gave the apostles witness of the resurrection of the Lord Jesus and great grace was upon them all" (Acts 4:33). This lightning rod of God's transforming presence was now being translated into the first-century church. They were telling the vision of what they had seen and heard on the mountain down below in the valley of decision, and great power was upon them.

When Stephen faced his persecutors as they opposed the message of Jesus, the Bible records, "And all that sat in the council looking steadfastly on him and saw his face as it had been the face of an angel." (Acts 6:15). Stephen's face shone with the same glory as Jesus had on the mountain. Suddenly it was not a private matter of a select few; it had become a worldwide event that reached out past every social and religious boundary with His message of eternal salvation. The awestruck disciples were now the carriers of His glorious presence into the uttermost parts of the earth.

We see now the engine of the gospel message that drives it into the world is His presence and glory. It is not a tantalizing self-induced experience that produces no fruit, but rather an illuminating light that leads the world to Jesus and becomes the pillar of fire that leads His church into the world. Yet often in contemporary circles, we see the opposite in effect. We want to privatize His glory and keep it shrouded in personal experience, assuming the world will simply catch on. But look at the words of Jesus carefully: "No man after he has lit a candle puts it in a secret place, neither under a bushel, but on a candlestick *so that they that come in may see the light"* (Luke 11:33, emphasis added).

"So that they that come in may see the light"—what are they coming into that a light is so important? They are coming into His kingdom like an airplane on a dark runway and need a spotlight guiding them to the shores of His presence and salvation! That's what He meant when it was declared prophetically, *"You* are the *light* of the *world."* (Matt. 5:14) *You* have become the transfiguring light of His presence and are the only hope of the world to see it: "To whom God would make known what is the riches of the glory of this mystery among the Gentiles, which is Christ in you, the hope of glory" (Col. 1:27). Why do we continue to try to light up heaven and become permanent fixtures there now? Do we think the Lord is limited of resources in heaven? Our job description now is to reveal the light of eternity in a dark world void of it. We will have ample time to be lights in heaven; right now we are lights to the world and here to transfigure and transform it.

Now we can see why He identified Himself as the Lord of the harvest. There was His crowning achievement, the joy set before Him and why He had suffered and died. It was the reason He was crucified to ransom lost mankind to Himself. He was the Lord of that harvest and had received an anointing and was now giving to His church the anointing to reap it.

The word *harvest* literally means "a reaping." In Luke 10:2, harvest is literally mentioned three times. A "reaping" is not going to be ready; it is already ripe, and the only hindrance to that reaping is the workers, or laborers. That word *laborer* can be interpreted in the ancient text as "toiler," or "teacher." This world needs someone to teach it the Word of God. As far as we appear to be climbing this current mountain of revelation and gifts, we can never disqualify the necessity of teaching and preaching His Word. It's the very reason the glory was given and that divine power was granted: to be His witnesses.

Look at Philip as he encountered the Ethiopian eunuch in Acts 8:26–39. Philip became the prophet to Africa's royal court, sent by God along the roadside. He became the teacher who illuminated the ancient text of Isaiah, revealing Christ to the eunuch. Then he was a mighty evangelist, who baptized the man in water along the way after the eunuch openly confessed, "I believe that Jesus Christ is the Son of God" (v. 38).

Rather than dissect God's power into cookie-cutter theologies, let's fully embrace the sheer power of His presence and step into the brilliant light of the Lord of the harvest and become his prophets, kings, priests, teachers, and evangelists to the world. In that exact moment, the world begins to press around us, like moths to the flame, as it did to Him and all of them then. We suddenly realize that we have entered a harvest that is a result of prophecy and have become the answer to His ancient prayer: "Pray then to the Lord of the harvest that He would send forth laborers into His harvest."

You become that laborer and you become that harvester, and the prophecy of Jesus of a great, glorious white harvest continues to unfold and be fulfilled. The harvest we face today is a prophetic one born on the winds of prophecy uttered from the mouth of Jesus two thousand years ago. Like Philip, run to it! You may see kings bow, princes baptized, and vagabonds saved. This great prophetic adventure awaits you, and His glory will carry you in the white light of His presence because you are a city upon a hill that cannot be hid, and you are the *leukos*, or light, of the world. Lord of the harvest, send them!

Epilogue

Where do you go from here? You have earnestly prayed, "Lord, here am I; send me." Now I want to present some practical directives to get you started. Your harvest and revival start *right now*. Every great endeavor started with one step forward and then the next and then the next. The moment you leave your home, your office, or your church today, you are God's emissary; and every saint from the beginning of creation peers from the banisters of heaven, watching you. You are not alone, as all the revivalists, missionaries, and evangelists of the ages are cheering you on. They, too, had one common denominator: to see the world saved and to cast their crowns of great achievement at His feet.

President Theodore Roosevelt said of these kinds:

It is not the critic who counts, not the man who points out how the strong man stumbled, or where the doer of deeds could have done better. The credit belongs to the man who is actually in the arena; whose face is marred by the dust and sweat and blood; who strives valiantly; who errs and comes short again and again; who knows the great enthusiasms, the great devotions, and spends himself in a worthy course; who, at the best, knows in the end the triumph of high achievement, and who, at worst, if he fails, at least fails while daring greatly; so that his place shall never be with those cold and timid souls who know neither victory nor defeat... The University of Paris, Sorbonne April 23, 1910

God does not need eloquent, polished arrows; He simply needs the rough, ruddy, cut-from-the-fabric-of-revival kind of soul that is willing and obedient. Look again at the city around you. Is their a convalescent home, a county jail, or halfway house? Look a little closer and you will find AA meetings and other places where the world congregates. If you refocus, you can see a myriad of opportunities pressing in from all around you. Bus depots are transformed from menial modes of transportation to hubs of harvest and evangelism. Every inconvenience becomes a divine appointment as you see the world through His eyes.

Suddenly the demand for elaborate buildings and high-dollar lease payments is eclipsed by parks, rivers, streets, and open, unconfined areas where people gather. Being a pastor is metamorphosed from mundane methodical ministry to an exciting backdrop full of surprises and danger. The title of evangelist is no longer a spiritual demotion in today's trophy case of achievements where the lost and dying are downgraded by yearly charities and checks in the mail. Suddenly the world becomes a great adventure, and the trail blazed by the great apostles of biblical proportions leads the charge. The lackluster attention given to outreach in the present conference scene is transformed by a vanguard of obedient foot soldiers who realize their greatest accomplishment in this life is to bring more joy to heaven than to Earth. You are His ambassador, and in a world where the laborers are few, your value is worth far more than gold!

As you pray that the Lord will use you, He will give you an inner compass of compassion that will lead you. Whether it is across the street or across the ocean, it will never fail you. His compassion will unlock every miracle, door, and opportunity. His love is the key into "the door of utterance" that Paul saw (Col. 4:3). He will shod your feet with the preparation of the gospel, and everywhere you go will be His possession.

You are a sent one, a shaft of light in a dark world that is your backdrop to love's perfection. He will immerse you into the crowd, as He did in His day, and you will do "greater works than these." You will be His Special Forces equipped for every good work as He transforms you into His evangelist and harvester. The world awaits you, and heaven stands at attention. Prepare yourself for eternity by what you give now, and the *cry of the harvest* will become your song too.

Chad Taylor
April 16, 2008

Consuming Fire Ministries

www.consumingfire.com

Please visit our website today for more crucial material to encourage and equip you for ministry. If you would like to invite Chad Taylor to your city, please visit www.consumingfire.com today.

Chad is also the author of the critically acclaimed book *Why Revival Still Tarries*. This book is available at our website, Destiny Image Publishers or a bookstore near you.

You can find many very useful revival tracts and material at www.lastdaysministries.org a ministry of Melody Green and the late Keith Green.